SPEAKING
—— WITH ——
AUTHORITY

SPEAKING
— WITH —
AUTHORITY

LES TOMLINSON, JR.

TATE PUBLISHING
AND ENTERPRISES, LLC

Published by Tate Publishing & Enterprises, LLC
127 E. Trade Center Terrace | Mustang, Oklahoma 73064 USA
1.888.361.9473 | www.tatepublishing.com

Tate Publishing is committed to excellence in the publishing industry. The company reflects the philosophy established by the founders, based on Psalm 68:11,
"The Lord gave the word and great was the company of those who published it."

Book design copyright © 2016 by Tate Publishing, LLC. All rights reserved.
Cover design by Samson Lim
Interior design by Gram Telen

Published in the United States of America

ISBN: 978-1-68301-490-4
1. Religion / General
2. Religion / Christian Life / Spiritual Warfare
16.03.09

Contents

Foreword

My first introduction to Les Tomlinson Jr. was a voice mail. He recently had an experience with God and felt that he was supposed to share his encounter with the church in the South Jersey area. He had called many churches but received almost no response. Meanwhile, I had been praying that God would teach me more about prophecy, specifically related to its use in His church today. It was no coincidence that Les called my office.

Since that day, I have benefited greatly from the friendship and spiritual relationship that has developed between us. Les has been a source of encouragement and education to me and the church, especially in the ministry of prophecy. Although I was already a pastor in a Pentecostal church, I understood very little about the special gift that Paul instructed believers to "earnestly desire." Les and I have spent hours in conversation and in prayer together eagerly desiring to hear the voice of God as He speaks to give instruction, direction, encouragement, correction, and wisdom in keeping with His Word.

I believe as you read this book, you will be guided into a better understanding of how God speaks and what He desires from His children. All authority belongs to Jesus, and in His wisdom, He has chosen to lend His authority to those who are called by His name. The responsibility to carry out God's will and purposes on the earth belongs to us, and we will stand before the Righteous Judge one day to give account of how we used it.

It is time to begin to correctly handle the Word of Truth that God has so graciously given in order to bring the light of the Gospel and make disciples of every nation. This book will teach you in a practical way what to do with the authority God has given you. But remember that you become responsible for what you know, so be prepared to begin to speak with authority.

—Lead Pastor Dan McAnney
Living Springs Global Fellowship
Hammonton, New Jersey

Introduction

Do you feel defeated at times? Are you tired of negativity interfering in your life? Do you feel that your children can do better but are not on the right path? Is your church suffering from gossip and slander? Have you noticed how the enemy is running amuck within the streets of your community? If you answered yes to these questions, then you have a great book in your hand to help you address them in Jesus's name!

There is a need in the church today to equip the saints to move in the authority we have been granted as ambassadors of Christ. Through this book, we will tackle who has the ability to speak with authority and how to enforce our victory in the Spirit!

We will travel down roads that will give us guidance, wisdom, and practical insight on how to dismantle the works of the enemy over your children, home, church, and community. It is time to take back what we have lost in the Spirit by exercising our authority in Christ.

Within these chapters, you will find tools to address the issues that you are facing today. As we venture through the Scriptures, you will be encouraged and inspired to set your feet on the right path to freedom!

It is time to break away from the substandard lifestyle we find in the church and address our enemy from a place of victory, not from a platform of fear! Buckle up and take a ride in the spirit that will break those chains around your life and bring the authority of Christ to earth through your declarations!

1

The Meaning of Authority

We will find within the church today that there are many views on what it means to have authority though Christ. Who has the ability to minister within that realm and how to implement it into our walk? Let's take a practical, insightful adventure in breaking down the meaning of spiritual authority and how we exercise it in our life today.

If we are going to speak, pray, and declare with authority, we must understand what authority is, correct? *Webster's Dictionary* defines *authority* as follows:

> : a citation (as from a book or file) used in defense or support *(2)*: the source from which the citation is drawn: a conclusive statement or set of statements (as an official decision of a court): a decision taken as a precedent *(3)*: power to influence or command thought, opinion, or behavior: freedom granted by one in authority: persons in command; *specifically*: convincing force.

Take a moment and think about this definition and the words that define what *authority* is and who has the right to enforce such power. First, it states that it is a *citation* from a book. The Bible is the *book* that we use in our teachings and intercession to declare the verdict given by our Righteous Judge—"We are not guilty!" Furthermore, we use the Word of God to *release a citation* to the enemy and enforce the victory that is ours!

Our words alone do not carry the authority. The anointing and the right to speak through the name of Jesus releases the ability to see the Gospel shared, the sick healed, demons flee, and the dead raised for His glory. As we step into the name of Jesus, standing as one with the Father, we become an instrument that echoes the voice of heaven.

As we engage heaven, seeking the heart of the Father, we disengage from the ways of the world and the thoughts of the enemy. We engage with our voice through faith to disengage spiritual opposition.

Another definition we find is *"power to influence."* This is an interesting definition! Who or what are we trying to influence? Our goal is to influence those who are lost and hurting in this world, to show them the way to salvation in Christ. Also, it may mean to enforce our "power of influence" over demonic strongholds. *(This does not mean we have the right or ability to change someone's will.)* This is where we enter into a spiritual battle against darkness and confess from a place of victory, seeking salvation for those who have not found the love of God (i.e., salvation.)

Our battle is in the heavenly realm, as seen in Ephesians 6:12 (NIV): "For our struggle is not against flesh and blood, but against the rulers, against the authorities, against the powers of this dark world and against the spiritual forces of evil in the heavenly realms."

We need to understand that to engage, we have to step into that realm through Jesus (John 10). To exercise authentic authority from heaven, we enter by faith through Jesus and release citations over the chaos we may be facing.

Even though we may see the effects of the battle unfold on earth, we need to become mature world changers and step on the field of battle through praise and understand that we enforce the victory in the heavenly realms. (See Daniel 10)

The last one to look at is *"freedom granted from one that is in authority."* Ultimately this is the Lord. Because He granted us salvation, we have the right and ability to lead others to a place of freedom through Christ.

It is so important for us to understand that if we are going to enforce what God has given us, we need to take a look at the way we speak to others, the way we pray, our view of our circumstances, and the prayers that are released over us.

The areas of authority that we are going to explore fall into four basic areas:

1. Preaching the Gospel
2. Laying hands on the sick for healing

3. Casting out demons or dealing within the spiritual realm

4. Raising the dead with the direction of the Lord

These areas of ministry are released by speaking and declaring with authority the *"will and purposes"* of the Lord over someone who is in need. As we minister in authority *(knowing who we are in Christ)*, we are basically releasing what the Father has granted in heaven. It is important to understand that it is not *our* authority we speak in, but the authority that was won for us on the cross and given from the resurrection! When we yield to the movement of the Holy Spirit, we will see these four areas of ministry working in us and within our sphere of influence.

It instead of *If*

What does this actually mean? Here is an example we may be able to relate to: Tim is sick and has asked some people to pray for him. (He is on the right path so far.) We have our dear sister Mary who starts out praying, and it goes something like this, "Dear Lord Jesus, *if it is your will* to heal Tim, please do so in Jesus's name."

Think about this prayer and mind-set. Does it align with the Word of God? To me, it could be offensive to our Lord Jesus. Why? The Bible states that by His stripes we *were* healed (Isa. 53:4–5)! How are we enforcing this promise or the victory we have in Christ over Tim's life? We're not!

If we are going to believe what is written in His Word and stand as ambassadors of Christ, we may need to change our speech, direction of prayer, and the perception of our authority in Christ.

When we pray *"If it is your will,"* how is that enforcing our victory? If anything, it is releasing doubt that Jesus is not capable to fulfill His own promise. He *is* our Healer, period! We must stop speaking negative words and praying over others with a lack of faith but in the power found in Jesus. I am not trying to offend anyone. I'm only trying to show that as we read the Bible, our prayers should align with the framework of the Scriptures. Our prayer and declarations must line up with the written Word to be effective!

One reason why there is such a lack of power demonstrated in the church today is due to the lack of faith as the Word is spoken or a prayer is released. We need to step above the ceiling of faith found today and ignore the standard being operated in the local church that is not being effective. We need to become a church that will grab hold of the altar of heaven, believing the fire of God to flow in us as we go and shine His love to the world.

Demonstration comes by faith and cooperation with the Holy Spirit. May faith arise in you as you declare the name of Jesus, being free in the spirit of God, learning how to colabor with heaven and the angelic host (Heb. 1:14).

A person speaking in authority knows what is right before the Father as they proclaim prayers inspired by the

Holy Spirit, seeing past what is before them and calling what lies ahead. They see spiritual life and decree it over that which is hurting (2 Cor. 4:13–14). The word *if* is not in the vocabulary of our Father in regard to His capability to fulfill His word or promises. He is *the* loving Father, and we must change our position in prayer. He *is* the God *"of all things are possible."* Nothing is too big for Him, so why are we praying prayers of *if* before the mercy seat?

We do not serve a God of *ifs*, for He is the Lord that is *able* to do whatever He so desires! Proclaiming a prayer with an *if* attached is like releasing a measure of defeat into the situation. Jesus defeated our enemy, so we must proclaim "it is your will, Lord" as we pray and allow God to have His way.

Operating in authority through Christ is declaring that Tim is healed by the stripes the Lord graciously bore for our sickness! We call Tim's body back to health and wholeness. We call his blood pressure to be normal. We call his white and red bloods cells to be at the perfect count as Christ created them be! There should be no ifs in our declaration. Instead, declare with an understanding that the Word of the Lord goes out and fulfills its purpose and does not come back void (Isa. 55:11).

Controlling Our Authoritative Actions

I believe this issue is close to the Father's heart. Authority is presented in two basic forms: speaking and the actions we portray in our walk. First, we will take a look at the speaking aspect of authority. It is our responsibility to harness our words and the way that we present them at all times. We should not allow our guard down whether we are speaking to an individual or to a hundred people. The end result is the same. Did we speak life or death to their heart, mind, and spirit?

In my years of ministry, I have heard people say "*I can not control my tongue. It has a mind of its own.*" I am not saying that I am perfect and never mess up (I would be lying), but I do try my best to govern my words and the attitude I walk in. If you are someone who struggles with controlling your words or, at times, abuse your authority while speaking to others, take a moment and confess this passage over your life:

> Those who guard their mouth and their tongue keep themselves from calamity. (Prov. 21:23, NIV)

In your prayer time, ask the Holy Spirit to put a guard over your mouth! As we continue to study the Word and allow it to burn within our bones, we will begin to speak with grace and not just spew out whatever we are thinking. The goal is to speak life into any situation; it is so easy to just say whatever comes to mind, but to move and speak in true authority, we must be aware of the words we are releasing and the consequences of our actions.

As we spend time soaking in the presence of the Lord, our vocabulary shall shift to resound the tone of heaven. The more time we spend listening to His voice and reading His Word, the more we become acquainted with the way He speaks. It should be our goal to speak the language of heaven as it reveals His authority through our voice box. Now that is exciting!

A person ministering kingdom authority understands and has respect for this position in the spirit and walks in the government of God. There are too many people who think they are ministering kingdom authority, but they are ignorant to the impact they are releasing with their words. Spiritual arrogance hinders the Holy Spirit and cancels out the glory of the Lord to be seen. Kingdom authority is granted and exercised through a faithful relationship with Jesus. There is a price that comes with spiritual authority. We need to lay down our thoughts and agendas and align ourselves with His will and purposes.

Authority is not exercising lip service by repeating fancy prayers before the Lord but having an attitude of reverence for our awesome God. We may speak, but the Lord fulfills the prayers we offer up! A simple example could be the difference between a rent-a-cop and a state trooper. A rent-a-cop has been given the right to represent themselves as an authority figure till a state trooper arrives on the scene, but the trooper has the right to declare the famous statement of authority: "You have the right to remain silent."

The same goes for us. To move in the power that is in the name of Jesus to govern the spiritual atmosphere around our life, we must have a solid foundation in Christ and not just be a Sunday-morning Christian. Do you want to be a spiritual rent-a-cop who just "represents" or a heavenly trooper who actually enforces authority and declares, "You have to be silent" to your enemy?

Genuine Authority

> For our appeal [in preaching] does not [originate] from delusion or error or impure purpose or motive, nor in fraud or deceit. But just as we have been approved by God to be entrusted with the glad tidings [the Gospel], so we speak not to please men but to please God, Who tests our hearts [expecting them to be approved]. For as you well know, we never resorted either to words of flattery or to any cloak to conceal greedy motives or pretexts for gain, [as] God is our witness. Nor did we seek to extract praise and honor and glory from men, either from you or from anyone else, though we might have asserted our authority [stood on our dignity and claimed honor] as apostles [special missionaries] of Christ [the Messiah]. (1 Thess. 2:3–6, AMP)

This passage is a great example that we must follow! Paul and Timothy understood the power and authority that they were given and were walking in as followers of Christ. They knew that their words carried authority and how it would impact the Thessalonians.

These men did not have any hidden motives for coming to Thessalonica but only wanted to spread the Gospel with purity. Neither should we go out with an impure heart or wrong motives. We must be on guard so that we do not fall into any traps of the enemy. When you are ministering, are you pleasing God or man? It is very easy to fall into the flattery of man. This will lead to abusing authority and could bring an end to your ministry. Flattery diminishes our authority, and we can lose respect of the brethren and, in turn, lose our position in ministry.

We must understand that our words will have a life-or-death impact on the one we are speaking to. If we fall into flattery, we are missing the mark and will become boastful in our own glory while applying the name of Jesus to our declarations.

Many fall into flattery because there is one important key component missing from their walk—love. Kingdom authority is solely given, established, and released from a heart of love. Without love, we are just clanging cymbals making a ruckus (1 Cor. 13:1).

Our ministry, confessions, and the prayers we offer should be in line with the passage above. We must always minister with a gentle spirit, a spirit of love that promotes the kingdom of God and not our own ministry desires. As we stand and minister in a state of humility, the Lord makes way for our ministry to flourish. The same goes for someone who has a desire to intercede for others, whether it is at an altar on a Sunday morning, at a prayer meeting, or for someone who is on a prayer team. Speaking with authority should always promote the heart of the Father!

Kingdom authority is found in Romans 14:17 (NIV), "For the kingdom of God is not a matter of eating and drinking, but of righteousness, peace and joy in the Holy Spirit." As you minister from the position of the royal priesthood, it should produce righteousness, peace, and joy inspired by the Holy Spirit and bring a change to the one you are speaking to.

Imagine a city changed because a believer stood up in faith and stepped into the name of Jesus, decreeing over the darkness that righteousness, joy, and peace must rule. Imagine people who proclaim the spiritual authority given within their birthright and demonstrating the power of the kingdom of heaven within the streets that are filled with darkness. Imagine a believer who goes to a council meeting in the spirit and speaks the intentions of God and decrees His wisdom over the wisdom of man and sees the answer unfold in the spirit realm and becomes real on earth.

A dear brother in Christ texted me one day asking for prayer for a family member who was being brought under false charges before the court. Things were not looking good for him. I said jokingly, "Hey, let's go to the meeting and speak the heart of God over those that are there?" You need to understand. The meeting was thousands of miles away from my home and was taking place the next day.

As I was at work the next day, I heard the Lord ask me if I was going to keep my word. I asked the Lord, "What word?" I had an urge to pick up my phone, and the first text message I saw was the one from my friend saying, "Let's go to the meeting." Instantly I said yes! Sitting at my desk, I said, "Father, by faith, I step into the name of Jesus as He is the door, and I will go to this meeting."

I found myself in the spirit going in a room with some men. I perceived I was in the meeting. I began to release the Father's love over this meeting and asked for Jesus the mediator to come on the scene and speak on behalf of my friend's family member. Two hours later, I received a text message, "All charges dropped!" This is what we should be doing—exercising kingdom authority on a daily basis!

Do not let your gifting get before you! Yes, our gifting makes way for a man, but if we abuse it, the Lord may stop revealing His secrets to us. Paul and Timothy ministered kingdom authority, but they did it in a way that was right before God. Even though they had to bring words of correction to the people, it was delivered in a way that was life to them and did not crush their love for the Lord.

Abusing Authority

Many years ago, I went to an open tent meeting. I was excited to go because I was so impressed with the church that was hosting the services. As the minister led the service, I could sense that he was a lover of Jesus, but something was lacking in his tone of speech. As the night went on, it seemed that he was more concerned with the crowd applauding him than reaching the hurt and lost souls around him.

When it came to the altar time, I decided to go up and receive whatever the Lord had for me that night. As I was standing there, I could hear this man yelling "godly" things to the people he was praying over, but I noticed that he was forceful in his actions.

Well, it was my turn to be ministered too. I was excited and believed that God was going to speak something to me and that I would leave that altar refreshed. Little did I know that I was in the line up to be pushed to the ground! As I stood there fighting his sweaty hands on my forehead, I began to get upset because this minister was so arrogant in the way he was trying to pray over me. It came down to me staring at him so he would get the message! God doesn't have to push people to get His point through. The minister moved on and continued to release his "zealous" prayers over the people next to me. A few moments later, he came back and tried the same approach, basically to get me to "fall under the power of the Holy Spirit." He leaned in and said these words: "You cannot receive from God because you are still standing."

Hello! Where is that in the Bible? I looked at him and said, "Stop trying to push people down thinking they are being touched by God." What he was doing was not the heart of the Father. I continued to explain to him that I can receive from God whether I am standing or lying on the ground, and if it is going to be on my back, then it will be from the touch of God and not him pushing me!

As he went on down the line, I noticed that his demeanor changed, and he was not pushing people down. His attitude and declaration in authority changed, and you were able to feel the Spirit of God being released. People were being touched, and I believe the will of the Lord was being fulfilled!

This man misrepresented kingdom authority as he was ministering to me and others. We must never mix our zealousness with authority. I am not saying, "Do not be excited before God." I love to be excited for the things God is doing, but we must harness our emotions while we are praying or exercising authority over others. *Your zealousness should not overcome your character.* Be free while ministering, but use wisdom.

What if I was not secure in my relationship with Christ and this man released those words to me that could have been devastating? This minister was the "authority figure for Christ in those meetings." I was trying to seek God and receive a touch from heaven, but I was told that I couldn't receive because I did not fall down!

See how a simple act of "immaturity" could have created a major separation between me and the Father? Who are we to be that judgmental? The minister did not know what was going on in my heart. What if I just became a Christian that night? What an awful thing to speak over someone. Authority ministered through "zealousness" could lead to a misrepresentation of true authority found in Christ.

It is so critical to understand that our words and the actions released while ministering within "authority" will penetrate whether we realize it or not. You may be speaking to someone that has put up a wall, and you think they are not listening. I am here to tell you, they will hear what you have to say. If it is negative, you can believe that the enemy will be there to aggravate the situation.

To close this story, let's say the minister was right. Maybe I was having a hard time receiving at that moment. The right thing that should have been prayed would be something like this: Father, have your way over this man. May he feel and receive the blessing of heaven. May your love pull down any wall around his heart and may the God of love be revealed to him tonight. Lord, I take authority over any darkness that is hindering this man's life and command all activity of the enemy to stop. I speak freedom to his mind, heart, and spirit to receive your love, in Jesus's name.

This prayer is saying the same thing, but it is not offensive. We have to think about what we are going to say or pray over someone to make sure that it is packaged in a way that it can be received. Remember, we are ambassadors of Christ. Yes, we may need to correct someone, but it must be spoken in love. You can deliver it in such a way that penetrates their heart and leads them to open up and receive His love. Speaking negatively could lead a man away from what God has intended for him.

Questions

1. Think about how you operate in authority within your prayer life. Are you speaking in faith, believing you have the right to speak to the negative things around your life?

2. If you are offended by an "if it is your will" prayer, think about the God we serve. He is the only God that can fulfill our prayers. Through God, all things are possible. If you pray this way, ask God to open your eyes so that you will have a deeper revelation of who He is. This will change the way you offer up your prayers. What are your thoughts on God still being able to heal today?

3. Think about your ministry or those around you. Have you given into any type of flattery? Have you opened a door to poof up your ego? Be honest with yourself, and if you have, repent and ask God to take away anything that is not of His Spirit.

4. Has your zealousness gotten in the way of your character? Think about your emotions and how they align with the character of Christ.

5. Have you been hurt by someone ministering to you? Have you been able to forgive them? Have their words hindered your walk? Remember, they may have had the right intentions but ministered them in a negative way.

2

In the Beginning

To start our journey to freedom and exercise our authority, we should take a trip back to the beginning of time in the book of Genesis. We will find one of the first things documented was God speaking things into creation! What an awesome thought. God spoke, and it came to be!

> For he spoke, and it came to be; he commanded, and it stood firm. (Ps. 33:9, NIV)

Thank you, God, for still speaking today! We need to establish a foundation to stand on in the spirit as we explore the power of our words and the effect they will have on someone's life, home, or community.

> In the beginning God created the heavens and the earth. Now the earth was formless and empty, darkness was over the surface of the deep, and the Spirit of God was hovering over the waters. And God said, "Let there be light," and there was light. (Gen. 1:1–3, NIV)

This passage illustrates the power of speaking and believing it to come to be. God saw the need for light, and he spoke it into existence! There are two things I would like to point out from this passage. First, God saw a need; second, He spoke out the result. Talk about power and authority being released! How many times have you had a need but never spoken to anyone or gathered a group of friends together, declaring the result?

We are able to see the issue at hand most times, but how many will believe, as we learn how to co-labor with heaven, that we have the result right before us? The result is found in Jesus, in that we need to seek the resources of heaven for the solution to the problem. If our faith is solely based on what we can see what man can provide, then we create a ceiling of expectation and will lack in receiving all the blessings of heaven for you, your family, your finances, your career, or your ministry.

Too many times, we think the small issues are not worth going before our Father. This is a snare many of us walk in. We decide to try to handle it on our own. Again, this is an offense to the Lord. He wants us to share *all* our burdens. Lean not on your own understanding! In trying to resolve spiritual issues without the leading of the Lord or the guidance of the Holy Spirit, we will miss the mark and will not receive the result—the blessings of the kingdom.

We must realize that God is just as concerned with our smallest need as He is with someone praying and calling forth their miracle or healing. It is the attitude of our heart that positions us before the Lord to receive. We should not just speak out (pray, call, and command) our needs for a miracle but express our daily needs before the Lord. Now we need to be careful. When we have a need that we keep presenting to the Lord without any action taken on our end, we could be praying amiss (James 4:3).

Our faith, hope, and belief play a role, whether we are asking God to heal a sore finger, supply food on our table, or provide a creative miracle. Faith is like gunpowder, and our prayers are like pulling the trigger of a loaded gun of heaven. The Holy Spirit takes our prayer (the bullet) and answers what we shot in the spirit realm. We need to understand that we must shoot in the spirit to affect the natural realm. Think about it. How assertive can we be without a loaded gun in a battle? The same is true in the spirit. We can ask, call things to align, and command the devil to flee, but we need to have faith *and* believe in Jesus to fulfill our petitions. In doing so, we must be okay with how He may answer us. Your prayers stir heaven to respond to the war cry birthed in your battle.

Some of you may be asking, "What do you mean, Les?" There can be times where we fall into complaining while we know the resolution to our need. Yes, God wants to hear the cry of our heart, but we need to be alert and respond to the answers we may receive either by His Word or by revelation. For example, if you know that you have to go to work to make ends meet but decide to stay home and ask the church to pray for God to meet your financial needs, this is an issue! We need to take ownership of our responsibilities and have the Lord direct us within them. Your voice is a weapon. Are you using it to better your life, or is it creating roadblocks out of immaturity of our understanding of its power?

This is a dangerous place to be. We do not want to abuse or misguide either the church or ourselves in prayer. The spirit world sees our actions, so heaven will assist if we are in right standing, or the enemy will come as a thief and rob your peace. If we try to speak to an issue in our life but ignore the reality that we are standing in, how can we expect the Lord to relieve us from that place? If you have to work (place of reality), then go to work! While you are there, call on the Lord for a new job if this one does not meet your needs. Speak to the circumstance. Release positive confessions in the spirit. Call on the favor of the Lord for a new job that is able to meet your needs.

Psalm 40:7–8 (NASB) says, "Then I said, 'behold, I come; in the scroll of the book it is written of me. I delight to do your will, Oh my God; your law is in my heart." Have you ever asked the Lord what has been scribed on the scroll that was written about you before you were formed? We need to refocus on how we pray and what we are seeking after. I rather spend ten minutes asking the right question than losing days, months, or even years praying amiss.

We need to awaken our prayer language as we engage heaven. There are supernatural realities waiting for us as we ask to see what has been set in the spirit before we ever walked the earth, but many times, we go through the day not seeing in the spirit because we don't ask or never even thought about doing so.

The passage in 2 Corinthians 10:6 (Mirror Translation) gives us a clear understanding of the language I am talking about. "Our ears are fine tuned to echo the voice of likeness that resonates within us. We are acquainted with the articulate detail of the authentic language of our origin." If we originate from heaven, then we should be acquainted with the language that is spoken there. This is not just for the heroes of the faith today but for all who call on the name of Jesus. It is our right to speak this language because we are the beloved of God!

I was praying one day, asking the Lord to reveal to me what has been scribed on the scroll about me because I thought it would be wise to go right to the source as the Lord holds the blueprint of my life. I was desperate to know what He had for this time in my life. Standing there with my eyes open, I saw a man in white linen walk through the wall and come and stand before me. I stood there in awe and holy fear of what I was experiencing, and he pulled out a scroll and opened it right before me!

I was so amazed with what was going on. I was lost in the presence of heaven that I became overwhelmed with bliss. As we made eye contact, he began to read off the scroll! He read what was on it, but the issue was, I couldn't hear his words! I asked a friend what this meant, and his opinion was that the Lord was speaking revelation into my life, and I had to go seek it out, and that is what I did. In doing so, great revelation came to me in the days and months after this encounter!

It is time to invoke heaven and its resources as we speak over our reality. One morning while heading to work, I stopped to make a cup of coffee. As I stood there making my coffee and trying to wake up, I had an open-eye vision. In this vision, I watched as a huge conveyor belt went before me. On it, there were presents, big and small in size, and then the vision left. Getting into my car, I asked the Lord, "What the heck was that, Father?"

I heard the Lord say, "They were all the blessings that I had for you, but you never asked for them."

Are you asking the Lord on a daily basis to release the blessings that are due to your name that day?

"The place of reality" we may find ourselves standing in should not shift our faith in the spirit realm. Our confession in the spirit should shift our position of *reality*. If we declare the negative position of reality, how can we stand strong in the spirit? We need to declare from a position of faith and victory to overcome our negative place of reality.

Some may ask, "How do I speak over my circumstances?" That brings us to the second point in this passage. God saw a need (light). He did not try to go around the need, but he spoke to the issue (darkness). There was darkness all around. God spoke light into the darkness! This is a great revelation the Lord gives us right in the beginning of His creation—speak into the darkness! Let the light of Jesus in you expose the darkness and destroy its hold over the issue at hand.

We need to take this passage and apply its principle in our daily walk. We must learn how to speak into the darkness that surrounds our life. *You* must learn how to take a stand and speak to the darkness and call the light of Jesus into your circumstances. Yes, we have a church body to support us, but there are times where you and you alone must address the enemy in your life.

We can gather as a family around each other to show support and seek revelation for the circumstance at hand, but there are times that you must enforce the authority the Lord has given you as an ambassador of Christ.

We must take advantage of this principle. As Christians, we have the assurance and ability to use the Scriptures as a weapon to defeat the circumstance. The Lord's will is for the betterment of the kingdom and His children. We must use the Word and speak to the issue we are facing from a place of "life" (i.e., victory) to see the negative mindset turn to a positive one that is focused on Jesus. Again, kingdom authority is from His throne, so we need to have a lifestyle that is focused on Him and not the works of the enemy around us.

One of the best ways the enemy keeps us at bay is to keep us from expressing our voice (*releasing prayers through authority*) in the battle. Many fall as a victim due to the fact they never take a stand and apply this truth in their walk. We must learn how to incorporate the Word of the Lord within our prayer life; our voice alone will not win the daily battles, but it is one vehicle to promote the kingdom of heaven around us.

> Do not let the members of your body lie around loose and unguarded in the vicinity of unrighteousness, where sin can seize it and use it as a destructive weapon against you; rather place yourself in readiness unto God, like someone resurrected from the dead, present your whole person as a weapon of righteousness. (Rom. 6:13, Mirror Translation)

This passage defines the way we are to present ourselves before the world—a weapon! We become a person as a weapon of righteousness. Your voice is like cannon in the war. As you release prayers and decrees that align with the written Word or are inspired by the Holy Spirit, they become like a cannonball hitting its target!

Words of righteousness are one of the keys to defeat that which is before you. Righteousness will not tolerate wickedness. It is time for the body to stand up and stop tolerating wickedness, whether it is being released by ourselves or those around us. We need to make a stand and disarm the voice of the wicked one and let the world hear the voice of truth! What voice will you allow to be heard louder? Will it be the voice of ISIS and other camps supporting the evil one? Or will you take a bold stand and declare righteousness over the land you stand on? Even Jesus promoted righteousness over wickedness.

> And Jesus entered the temple and drove out all those who were buying and selling in the temple, and overturned the tables of the money changers and the seats of those who were selling doves. And He said to them, "It is written, 'MY HOUSE SHALL BE CALLED A HOUSE OF PRAYER'; but you are making it a ROBBERS' DEN." (Matt. 21:12–13, NASB)

The question is, Will you stand in the house of prayer over fellowship in the robbers' den? Are you becoming aware that the Father is looking for you to make a stand by opening your mouth and calling on the Holy Spirit and asking the Lord to release the angelic host to come and battle with us, or are you wrapped up in the daily affairs of life and don't see how you can make a difference? Beloved, one glance from you makes His heart beat faster (Song of Sol. 4:9)! Please don't give into the lie anymore that you have to be a leader to bring change, but be encouraged that you were created to be a part of His great plan to show the world His loving-kindness!

I once heard a musician say, "I need a voice larger than mine." As we declare from our position in the heavens, Jesus seconds the petitions that align with the will and purposes of the Lord. You may have seen the picture of a boy acting big and strong to scare off his bully, not knowing that his daddy was behind him. The bully was scared because the boy's daddy was standing behind his son all along. It is the same for us in the spirit realm. When we "flex our muscles," the enemy runs because Christ backs up the prayers and declarations that bring life! It is at the name of Jesus the enemy flees, not in the name of you or me.

> Whoever acknowledges me before others, I will also acknowledge before my Father in heaven. But whoever disowns me before others, I will disown before my Father in heaven. (Matt. 10:32–33, NIV)

I truly believe that the Lord could have created the light into the darkness by means other than speaking, but I believe He did it to set a principle for us to live by. The coupling of the voice and the actions we take are as powerful within the spirit as they are within our daily walk on this earth, but we must learn how to uncap this power and exercise authority!

The Light Pole

Can we speak light into darkness? We know that we are not God and are not able to actually create light, but we are able to call on the Lord, and He loves to perform the impossible. Also we are vessels of His power. He is waiting for us to understand that we are access points of heaven on earth. How so?

> In Him you are co-constructed together as God's permanent spiritual residence. You are God's address! (Eph. 2:22, Mirror Translation)

Being His address, just think about the power that can flow out of your mouth, but you must be willing to step up and take the jump of faith that comes with risks. In doing so, you begin to transform that which has been covered in darkness to produce fruit of heaven! We are one with the Lord, so He speaks through us. Talk about kingdom power and walking in His authority, wow!

I would like to share this little story that took place in my life. I can remember it so clearly to this day. I was struggling with some issues in my life and couldn't enter into the breakthrough I needed. As I was praying, in my silliness, I said, "Lord, show me that you are there and are able to take me out of this pit!" There was a street pole with a light that rarely came on in front of my home, so I asked the Lord to turn the light on as a sign that He heard my prayers, and I was able to experience freedom from this struggle. No sooner had I said amen than the old light came on and shone for a few minutes and then went off. God meets us where we are at! Now I am not saying that we should test the Lord, but that is where I was at, and He showed His love as He will do for you. Are you turning to the Father, believing His goodness is for you, or are you suffering because you don't realize the power as you speak to the darkness that seems so heavy around you?

My reason for sharing that story was to express to you that I had to speak, seek the Lord in prayer, and call His light to shine in the darkness. I was full of hope and excitement when that happened. It was like, "Wow, my God hears my prayers!" The devil surely did not like that victory. Are you ready to walk in your victory? Beloved, make a stand before the courts of the Lord and ask the Righteous Judge to release a cease and desist sentence to your enemy! Ask Jesus to stand in the court with you as your mediator and speak on your behalf (Rom. 8:34)!

Questions

1. Think about an issue that you are dealing with. Are you going to the Lord only with your major problems, or do you present all your burdens to God? If so, take some time and repent and ask God to forgive you for not trusting Him with *all* your burdens.

2. Are you speaking out negative words over your situation (e.g., "I will never get out of this hole," "That's just my luck," "Things never go well for

me")? If so, you must take ownership of these words and repent. We can become what we speak. As you speak positive things, you should walk in a positive state of inner peace even through trials.

3. How are you dealing with your "place of reality" and your inward peace? Is it controlling you, or are you controlling it by your confessions of faith?

3

Speaking Life

In this chapter, we will look at releasing *life* into our spiritual walk. The opposite of life is *death*. Life and death produce fruit. Which fruit is being released out of your mouth today? As we venture through this chapter, I encourage you begin to meditate on Proverbs 18:20–21. Ask the Lord to bring revelation to your spirit on how the fruit you may be walking in can and will affect the atmosphere! The foundation of this book is found in the following passage.

> From the fruit of their mouth a person's stomach is filled; with the harvest of their lips they are satisfied. The tongue has the power of life and death, and those who love it will eat its fruit. (Prov. 18:20–21, NIV)

Our spiritual authority should be exercised from a foundation created from the passage above. "The power of life and death" lies within your tongue. The latter part of this scripture is really never quoted. This may happen when someone is trying to use a verse to fit within their circumstance or mind-set. (Please study the context of a passage and apply it in the right manner, or the enemy will have a field day in your thought process.)

It is hard enough to comprehend that life and death are released from our tongue, but then factor in "those who love it will eat its fruits," meaning if you love speaking life (i.e., blessings, uplifting words, and encouragement), you will eat of its fruit! The opposite side of this coin is, if we are speaking death (i.e., slander, gossip, anger, and disrespect), then you will eat the fruits of death!

Proverbs 16:21 (NASB) says, "The wise in heart will be called understanding, and sweetness of speech increases persuasiveness." Being a representation of Christ on earth, we should be known as men and women who are "wise in heart." The world is looking to see what you will say and how you will speak when trials arise. How are you going to speak to the storm before you? Will you be wise and speak from the heavens in faith or be a part of the epidemic we see in the body today and buckle under pressure? I want to see a people rise up and be called understanding and be known for their sweetness of speech!

If we are going to be a people that want to bring cultural transformation, we will need to learn how to speak in the heavens and take trips in the spirit to other geographical places (led by the Holy Spirit) as we exercise and walk in authority on earth. Transformation will be birthed through colaboring with heaven and walking out in what we receive from the Father. Our speech must birth the fruit of persuasiveness!

Releasing Life through Your Words

Then God said, "Let us make mankind in our image,
in our likeness, so that they may rule over the fish
in the sea and the birds in the sky, over the livestock
and all the wild animals, and over all the creatures
that move along the ground." So God created
mankind in his own image, in the image of God he
created them; male and female he created them.

—Genesis 1:26–27 (NIV)

God spoke mankind into creation! Now we understand that we cannot speak a human into creation. Don't give in to the lies of the devil and weird theology. We have the ability to speak life over the womb! When my wife was pregnant, we would speak (pray and declare with authority) over our little baby, that she would have a genuine love for Jesus and walk in her purpose of creation. At a very young age, she would express her desire for the things of God and love to worship the Lord. Of course, we asked for the Father's heart about our babies and set our prayers in accordance to what we felt, heard, or saw in the spirit about them.

I must say, I am a very proud daddy of two beautiful girls. They both have such a gentle, loving character and care for others. Did our prayers have anything to do with this? Absolutely! The same applies for yours over your family. Makayla loves to sing and worship, and at only three years old. I believe that she will be one who has wisdom before her years. I believe that her love for things of God are twofold. One, it could be the call the Lord has on her life. Second, we prayed and spoke life over her soul as she was in the womb and continue to do so nightly as we tuck her into bed! We do the same for our beautiful Shelby Grace.

We must speak, pray, and declare with authority (the assurance that we can move mountains) life over your children. Become fearless in the spirit of God for the welfare of your children. If don't have any, then over your job, ministry, or family. Make a stand for your family—may we stop waiting for chaos to happen before we see in the spirit realm. Will you believe that you can make a stand in the spirit and see what is coming and have faith in knowing that you can speak to it, whether it is a movement of God or a plan of the enemy?

> I will stand on my guard post and station myself on the rampart; And I will keep watch and see what He will speak to me and how I may reply when I am reproved. (Hab. 2:1, NASB)

May we not make excuses and say that this is the role solely for an intercessor. We should have a prayer life that stands at the post of our home and watch the movement in the spirit so we know to align or dismantle the waves in the atmosphere around us and our family!

Our actions, prayers, and decrees set the standard for the legacy we will leave behind. Pray scripture over their walk. Pray that they fulfill the call and purposes that are before them—not what the world has to offer but what was written about their lives before they were formed. If we do not take ownership of our children, then we have given them into the hands of the world! Who do you want speaking into your life, over your family, your job, your church, or your community? If we, the church, do not step up to the plate, the enemy is right there to speak into their ear and derail them from the purposes of God.

This principle applies in other areas of our life also. We need to become not just stewards but great stewards of what the Father has given us—yes, what He "has given" because He is a good Daddy and knows the fullness of your potential in life. May we become people who stop listening to the lies around us and become dreamers of the greater good—transformation for the sake of the kingdom of God!

Your prayer life truly assists with the direction and impact you will have on your surroundings. Imagine leaving a legacy that continues to bring an impact for the generations to come. May our legacy be known to others as people who moved in power, co-labor with heaven, and understood how to walk in the authority of Christ even as our speech was sweet, persuasive, and effective in transforming the darkest areas of society.

> For we are God's [own] handiwork [His workmanship], recreated in Christ Jesus, [born anew] that we may do those good works which God predestined [planned

> beforehand] for us [taking paths which He prepared
> ahead of time], that we should walk in them [living
> the good life which He prearranged and made ready
> for us to live]. (Eph. 2:10, AMP)

That verse sets the tone for our intercession as we pray over our children, the wayward son or daughter, the newly converted Christian, or those who have not yet come to the place of repentance. Become alert to hearing the voice of the Lord and the leading of the Holy Spirit. We don't need to wait to be in a prayer meeting to exercise intercession.

I had an encounter with the Lord as I meditated on what was intercession and how to go about doing it throughout the day. I heard the Lord say, "Intercession is just that. It's an inter cession with Him." The Father loves simplicity. The church would grow faster if our teachers would learn how to minister in just that—simplicity. (Yes, I understand that some revelation is deep and needs time to process—be yourself!) In that meeting, we gain insight of the Father's heart toward the one we are praying for. He leads us to speak in boldness over chaos, destroying misunderstandings, apathy, confusion, and delusion, and begins to show us how to wage war in the heavenlies with the Sword of His Spirit, which is the Word! Let's become people who have numerous inner meetings with the Lord on a daily basis—and, yes, even at work or as you are driving, cooking, or doing yard work.

We have the ability to "call and decree" (Eph. 2:10) into its fullness over the one we are praying for. As we begin to understand that the Word of the Lord is alive and active, we need to exercise our authority and see heaven meet earth. Many people are on the path of destruction, but we are able to pray that they would walk down the path that God has ordained for them to follow before their creation. Remember what is on the scroll of their life (Ps. 40:7–8). In your intercession, ask the Lord to reveal what is scribed for today and then prophesy it over them!

We can not change someone's will, but we can ask the Holy Spirit to convict them and show them the love of the Father wherever they are in life. We can pray for them and call the reality of this passage to come to past and destroy the yokes of the enemy. Speak kind words to them and show the love of the Lord. You are an access point of heaven for them to encounter His loving-kindness. Will you open yourself up and let the wind of heaven breathe life to those you stand before? You are the instrument of heaven that is being used to voice His good intentions for those in chaos. Become bold in your declarations.

> Pleasant words are honeycomb, sweet to the soul and healing to the bones. (Prov. 16:24, NASB)

Some have taken a stance in the church that ministering in kingdom authority has to be stressful, loud, and overbearing. You might have witnessed someone praying to disengage the enemy from his hold on a person. For some reason, I have noticed many in the church think the devil is deaf, so they yell at the top of their lungs, "Come out!" and become aggressive in their conduct. Is this necessary?

I believe we can move in authority and control our conduct. Do I believe there will be times that we get excited in our prayer? I sure do. But let's not make it a way to teach or think we have to be so loud every time we enter in. Kingdom authority can be exercised through kind words that break strongholds. Jesus is love—these are some of the kindest words we will ever speak over some one, but they are also some of the most powerful words that we can deliver.

Speaking in authority should produce fruit that brings healing to our bones! Did Jesus raise His voice? I am sure He did, but did He have to every time He prayed over an individual or crowd? Let's be sensitive in the spirit and speak words that are like the honeycomb that gives life! There is nothing wrong with a prayer full of zeal as long as it is based in love and emanates the heart of the Lord.

We need to become more aware as we pray or stand up and speak under the authority of Jesus; we are invoking the supernatural realm! Our words pierce through the atmosphere and are being heard by the King of kings. The enemy knows this, and that is why many struggle in their prayer life. If the enemy can see your plan of attack (*prayer, declaring in authority*), wouldn't you think that he will try to corrupt your mind-set on how powerful you really are in the Spirit?

Here is the meaning of *confidence* from *Webster's Dictionary*:

1. Faith or belief that one will act in a right, proper, or effective way <have *confidence* in a leader.

2. A feeling or belief that you can do something well or succeed at something.

3. A relation of trust or intimacy.

Become confident in who you are as being the beloved of God! The authority through Christ destroys the works of the enemy, period!

> Scripture is clear, "Abraham believed what God believed about him and that concluded his righteousness." (Rom. 4:3, Mirror Translation)

May we become confident like the model Abraham set before us! The body of Christ needs to stand up and truly speak with boldness to the storms that are upon this world. We have been given the keys of the kingdom. Now we need to begin to unlock the mysteries of His authority and see darkness dismantled in the midst of our prayers.

Believe in what God says you are. If He is a roaring lion (lion of Judah, the one that can open the scrolls, Rev. 5:5), then you become a roaring lion that walks in the knowledge of its power within the framework of humility. He is the King of kings (the little *k* is for those who follow

Him). Become one who speaks like a king, with authority, direction, clarity, and boldness, someone who will not back down till that which is started is finished for the sake of the kingdom. Remember, confidence and kingdom authority is founded in love and intimacy with Jesus.

Another point about confidence is found in Romans 4:21 (Mirror Translation), "Abraham's confidence was his dress code, he knew beyond doubt that the power of God to perform was equal to His promise." What an amazing passage! We must never leave home without checking our dress code. Are you walking in confidence today as you pray? Some of us may lack in our prayer life because we are not confident in ourselves or in the one we are praying to. Being a Christian, we have accepted the role of being a warrior in His great army. A warrior knows that there is not a ceiling of confidence. If we get complacent in the battle, then we will see spiritual casualties. Furthermore, we must believe in the authority that we speak in. If we are speaking to chaos, then we must not doubt the power of God to show up!

Still today, there are many Christians who speak with negative overtones in their declarations and prayer life, even in the church community and at times right from the pulpit. For an example, let's say Bobby has backslidden. I've heard so many statements like, "Oh, he will never change," and in the next breath, they pray, "Dear Jesus, touch Bobby in a special way." Now if I were Bobby and heard that conversation, I would think these people were confused! They are confessing Bobby will never change, releasing death, but then also seeking life from heaven. The two do not mix!

Yes, God is more than able to captivate Bobby and draw him toward His love, but why are we sitting around declaring that Bobby will never change? Your negative declaration is cancelling out your authority in prayer. Doesn't that prayer contradict their confession? Think about what you are confessing. If it is not positive, do not release it!

Questions

1. What does Proverbs 18:20–21 state?

2. Have you become aware of your confessions? Are they life or death?

3. We cannot change someone's will, but have you changed the way you are praying for them?

4. Do you believe in what God believes about you?

5. Have you performed a dress code check today? Where is your level of confidence?

4

Speaking Death

God spoke the initial words of life into existence as the enemy spoke the first words of death to mankind. This should be a guideline in exercising authority: we need to speak life to that which seems dead. We should always use the written Word first to address the issue we are faced with!

Matthew 4 sets this principle in motion. We see Jesus being tempted by Satan. After being tempted on three different occasions, Jesus made the following statement, "As it is written." We should pay attention to this statement as Jesus Himself used it multiple times in His defense, which is actually the role of offense! As we grow in moving within kingdom authority, we need to make sure we have the written Word as part of our arsenal.

One other point I want to make from Matthew 4 is found in verse 11 (NASB), "Then the devil left him; and behold angels came and began to minister to Him." When the tempter or death itself is knocking on your door, it is perfectly okay to ask the Holy Spirit and the angels to come and minister to you. This is a key that the body of

Christ is not walking in as many think that this is likened to worshiping the angels. Absolutely not! We only worship the Lord Jesus! If Jesus Himself needed to be ministered to by angels, how much more would we need this? Also read Hebrews 1:14 as they are there to serve those that believe in Jesus!

> Now the serpent was more crafty than any of the wild animals the LORD God had made. He said to the woman, "Did God really say, 'You must not eat from any tree in the garden'?" The woman said to the serpent, "We may eat fruit from the trees in the garden, but God did say, 'You must not eat fruit from the tree that is in the middle of the garden, and you must not touch it, or you will die.'" "You will not certainly die," the serpent said to the woman. "For God knows that when you eat from it your eyes will be opened, and you will be like God, knowing good and evil." (Gen. 3:1–5, NIV)

The above passage has been known as "The Fall of Mankind" within the Christian community as man jeopardized his relationship with God by eating the forbidden fruit from the tree in the middle of the garden. Who led Eve to the fruit? How was she deceived? The serpent "*spoke*" to her, twisting the words of the Lord in such a way that she did not see anything wrong with what the serpent spoke in regard to the fruit.

The enemy still uses this scheme today. It is important that we understand the Word of the Lord and study it so we know what the Bible says as we learn how to apply it on a daily basis! We are held accountable for the actions we take. You have to make the time to study the Word so you do not get tricked like Eve and partake in the fruits of death.

> For every person will have to bear [with patience] his own burden [of faults and shortcomings for which he alone is responsible]. (Gal. 6:5, AMP)

As the Lord *spoke* the first words of life and the enemy *spoke* the first words of death, what words are you allowing to direct your path today? Are you eating the fruit of life or the fruit of death? This passage shows us the true meaning of eating the fruit of death.

What fruit (curse, death) did the serpent, Eve, and Adam partake in regard to the trickery and disobedience to the Lord?

> So the LORD God said to the serpent, "Because you have done this, "Cursed are you above all livestock and all wild animals! You will crawl on your belly and you will eat dust all the days of your life. And I will put enmity between you and the woman, and between your offspring and hers; he will crush your head, and you will strike his heel." To the woman he said, "I will

> make your pains in childbearing very severe; with painful labor you will give birth to children.
>
> Your desire will be for your husband, and he will rule over you."To Adam he said, "Because you listened to your wife and ate fruit from the tree about which I commanded you, 'You must not eat from it,' "Cursed is the ground because of you; through painful toil you will eat food from it all the days of your life. (Gen. 3:14–17, NIV)

The serpent (our enemy) tricked Eve into eating the apple by deceiving her through a form of trickery (speaking with the intent to deceive.) How is trickery being used against us today? The dictionary defines *trickery* as "the practice of crafty underhanded ingenuity to deceive or cheat." It is so imperative to know the Word of God just on this mere fact. There are some many people walking the earth who are hurt or being led astray and whose lives are being destroyed due to the art of trickery. Trickery is found in the church community because we have let our standards down. We must recognize it and disarm the works of the enemy.

May we not let the beloved of God walk around in a daze any longer, even more so those that don't know the love of Jesus. All of us know people who are misled, confused, or downright taken advantage of. What are we going to do about it? Remember we want to leave a legacy that is known about our sweet but powerful words. It is time to remind the sting of death that is has no hold unless we hold on to it ourselves (1 Cor. 15:55).

The Serpent

In verse 14 of Genesis 3, the Lord cursed the serpent, and it would crawl upon its belly all its days, eating dust. The Lord said he would put enmity between the serpent and mankind. What is enmity? The dictionary says, "Typically mutual hatred or ill will." This is true today. Many people do not like snakes in any manner or form. Many say they are scared of them and do not want to be around any kind of snake. I never came across a snake I liked or one that I would want to have in my home. (No ill will to those that like snakes!)

Many years ago, my sister was taking care of our neighbor's horse while they were out of town. One day while attending to the horse, she saw a snake in the barn. She did what most young girls would do—ran back home yelling, "There is a snake in the barn!" Our dad went over there to take care of the issue. As he entered the barn, he saw the snake as it was hissing at him. He did not think twice about what he did next. He found a hoe (weapon, just like your words) and went to battle with the snake (our tempter, enemy) and cut its head off (victory). He disarmed the attack! Why do I share this? The latter part of verse 15, "He will crush your head, and you will strike his heel."

What does this mean? This is the first time we see a "battle" in the Scriptures. We must realize that there is a spiritual battle going on in and around our lives. This verse is a key to understanding that the Lord has given us the victory to stand on. Yes, you may be in a situation where you cannot see the light, but you must speak to the issue and let the darkness know that your Lord will crush its head! Please remember, you are the vessel He uses to thwart the attack of the enemy. As your words align with His readiness to release His power, angels, or ministry of Holy Spirit, there is a collision in the spirit realm, and our victory is the result.

Now we need to understand that just because we don't see the victory in a moment's notice doesn't mean that battle isn't won. As the battle is being disarmed in the heavens, we need to stay aware of the lies that will try to undermine our faith, belief, and authority. Many fall away because they can't see. If the supernatural was all based on seeing, that would be great, but it's not. (Faith opens up the seeing eye into the supernatural.) There is a level of faith we stand in as we declare from a place of kingdom authority.

> Jesus said to her, "Did I not say to you that if you believe [in Me], you will see the glory of God [the expression of His excellence]?" (John 11:40, AMP)

Some may ask, How do we speak against the battle? The striking of the heel is the enemy trying to attack and derail you from your potential. If the enemy can get to your "feet" (which is a part of our armor, symbolic to peace in Eph. 6) it will impact your direction and could lead you or your family into disarray. Many actions that we act upon are in reflection to the words that are spoken over us. If you listen to what is said on a daily basis around your life and evaluate the difference between life and death, what side of the fence would you find yourself on?

> The dynamic of our strategy is revealed in God's ability to disengage mindsets and perceptions that have held people captive in pseudo fortresses for centuries! (2 Cor. 10:4, Mirror Translation)

Through Jesus, we find the key to disengage false mindsets. As we turn to Him and ask for clarity, He is so willing to meet with us and show us the way out. The question is, Do you want the way out, or do you like the attention you gain through the struggles you walk in? Even though that may sound odd, the fact is that there are many hurting beloved children of God holding on to their sickness, struggles, or disappointments because they are being led by a lie that says, "This is how you will be accepted." Friends, we need to take back this area in the church and stand in our position of authority in the spirit and begin to cast every lofty idea into the abyss so others can walk in the freedom we hear about in the name of Jesus.

The words we surround ourselves with (i.e., music, TV, the Internet, books, or friends) have a major role in the direction we will walk in on a daily basis or the uncertainly of walking into the unknown that lies before us. We must take captive the negative thoughts, actions, and words that come at us and those we release over others. If not, we are giving way and allowing the enemy to strike our heel, causing our demise.

Mankind

The disobedience of Eve led Adam to disobey the Lord. We can see the consequences that man will have to endure to the Second Coming of Christ. Adam and Eve were spotless before God and walked naked in the garden because they knew no sin. This book is about the power and authority in our words so we will not venture down the road of disobedience created by their actions. However, we needed to bring clarity about the serpent and why it is imperative to study the Word and have it burning brightly in our walk.

In closing, I do believe that we can walk again in the garden of the Lord. Once we confess that Jesus is our Lord and Savior, we need to go past the traditional mind-set of "sinner saved by grace" as that is the launching pad to the place where we stand today as expressed in 2 Corinthians 5:21 (AMP), "He made Christ who knew no sin to [judicially] be sin on our behalf, so that in Him we would become the righteousness of God [that is, we would be made acceptable to Him and placed in a right relationship with Him by His gracious lovingkindness]."

The mind-set of death makes us believe that the cross was our finishing point. Yes, we get to go to heaven for eternity. Thank you, Jesus. I would like to challenge you that the cross was the starting point for our walk on the earth. We need to walk with the attitude that we became the righteousness of God. If we do so, He will not be far off with a bat in hand to whack us each time we slip into the sinful nature. No, He is a gracious God that sees us as His sons and daughters and not some sinful being that needs discipline every day.

Speaking negative words and walking with a bad attitude creates a lifestyle of one having a slave mentality, but speaking and standing with a positive attitude creates a lifestyle of one being a son of God. Romans 8:15 (Mirror Translation) makes this point so clear for us: "Slavery is such a poor substitute for sonship! They are opposites; the one leads forcefully through fear while sonship responds fondly to Abba Father."

Questions

1. Think about the words you use on a daily basis. Do you see or feel that you have any involvement speaking negativity to your children, family members, peers, or coworkers? If so, take some time

and repent. Ask God to help with putting a guard over your mouth!

2. Do you feel that you have entertained trickery or that others have used it against you? If so, you must forgive those who have hurt you in any way, first and foremost. Secondly, use your authority to break the bonds that are holding you down. Destroy the works of negativity that have been spoken over you. Remember, we serve a living God that won the victory when He died on the cross. It is up to us to enforce that victory today!

3. Think about the way you speak. How do your words affect others? Are you lifting them up or tearing them down? Remember, life and death are in the power of your tongue, and those who love it will eat its fruit.

4. Have you read any scripture today? Remember, we need to study the Word so we know how to combat the enemy and how to seek out false pretense by those who will try to use trickery within the church.

5. Do you see yourself as a sinner or the righteousness of God?

5

Abomination

When you hear the word *abomination*, what comes to mind? I think the worst. It is such a strong word, and it is not used often within today's social vocabulary. *Webster's Dictionary* defines it as "extreme disgust and hatred." I would say they are pretty strong words, wouldn't you agree?

Why do I bring this up? What does this have to do with speaking or moving in the realm of authority? We are still establishing the foundation to stand on within the realm of speaking with authority. Within doing so, it is my goal to cover the major aspects related to speaking while keeping it simple!

> Haughty eyes, a lying tongue, And hands that shed innocent blood, A heart that devises wicked plans, Feet that run rapidly to evil, false witness who utters lies, And one who spreads strife among brothers. (Prov. 6:17–19)

Imagine a society that uses this passage as a standard to be upheld. Think about how enjoyable it would be to live in peace with everyone. We know that the enemy is on the prowl to take down anyone who gives way to his wrongdoings or believes in the lies he creates around us. This passage is a *standard* that we as Christians need to follow. I am not saying that Christians break this standard on a daily basis just to be spiteful, but I have seen some in action leading people to the point of breaking them spiritually, being abusive, and ultimately driving members of the body of Christ to walk away from their faith. At that point, we have lost a soldier for Christ, and the enemy has a temporarily won. True repentance, authority, and the love of Christ can restore what was lost. He is still our hope!

In breaking this passage down, there are seven things that are an abomination to God. Remember earlier we talked about the two basic ways authority is presented to an individual? One, in the realm of speaking and, second, the actions we portray. Three abominations derive from someone speaking:

1. Lying tongue

2. False witness

3. Someone who spreads strife among brothers

I want to be clear. This is not to judge anyone but to bring an awareness to a believer who is walking in a way that is not pleasing to the Lord. Yes, there is a difference between having a sinful nature and finding oneself in a situation that leads into doing wrong. Repentance is the key! Once you noticed you are doing wrong, repent, ask God to reveal the truth in the situation, and move on. Do not let the enemy keep you in darkness. We have a voice. It's time to purposely use it against the enemy. We must stop using it against our own families, friends, church, and, ultimately, ourselves.

God views these abominations with "*extreme disgust*" and "*hatred*." Out of these three abominations, I would say the one that a Christian falls into the most would be "one who spreads strife among brothers." The enemy has been causing strife between brothers since the fall (Cain and Abel or Joseph and his brothers, for example). His goal is to destroy any relationship that is rooted in the love of our Father, Jesus Christ.

I've heard stories about gossiping that created such disunity to the point that people actually disowned a fellow believer in Christ. Is this right for either side? Of course not! Please understand that your words and actions speak volumes in the spirit realm and not only in the natural. (*Remember, our battle is not with flesh and blood, even though many seem to feel that is what they are wrestling with.*) You might think that you are just "talking" about someone's issue; however, the enemy is using it to bring destruction to the one who is suffering, hurting, or walking in a sinful nature.

May we not be so foolish with our words. We need to think before we speak! Is this conversation going to lift up my brother or sister, or is it going to hinder them? Just because you are speaking in "secret" with someone about another person does not mean that your words are not being heard. You have an enemy that takes what he hears and torments the one who is suffering. You may think that the one you are speaking to in "secret" (first mistake) is strong enough to control their tongue (second mistake). What if they go off blabbing their mouth and spreading rumors, lies, and gossip about what was said? You are just as guilty as the one gossiping because you started a conversation that should have never existed, and that has ramifications in the spirit and natural realm.

> Make a tree good and its fruit will be good, or make a tree bad and its fruit will be bad, for a tree is recognized by its fruit. You brood of vipers, how can you who are evil say anything good? For the mouth speaks what the heart is full of. A good man brings good things out of the good stored up in him, and an evil man brings evil things out of the evil stored up in him. But I tell you that everyone will have to give account on the day of judgment for every empty word they have spoken. For by your words you will be acquitted, and by your words you will be condemned. (Matt. 12:33–37, NIV)

What does this have to do with kingdom authority? It's called *negative* authority. If you cannot control your words, you will become a hindrance to others, and the enemy will help you think that you are doing well for the kingdom of God. Remember the old statement your parents would say,

"If you do not have anything nice to say, don't say anything at all." Many Christians still struggle with this today. Yes, I mean our brothers and sisters in Christ! I believe many of them do this because it makes them feel "accepted" by others, meaning if they talk about someone else (and not deal with their own issues), they portray it as *wisdom* but in reality, it is called *gossip* and immaturity.

Proverbs 20:19 sheds light on this: "He who goes about as a slanderer reveals secrets, Therefore do not associate with a gossip." May we become aware of who we associate with and the impact we are having on them and how their words direct our conversations. We want to be known as people who guard our hearts and do not get tangled up with gossip. This goes even within family matters. The principle is the same across the board—stay away from slander and gossip.

Being in ministry, you hear a lot of things. At some point, you have to make a decision to ignore what is being said, address it, or continue along the path of slander that is being set before you. Many ministers want to think that their conversations about others are healthy. Well, if it is about a person's negative side, then it's not at all. Of course, I am not talking about discussing an issue that might come up, but we need to be wise in how far we allow the conversation to go.

As a Christian, we have been given the authority to spread the Gospel and release wisdom, revelation, and knowledge. We have also been given the ability to pull down strongholds. The Bible doesn't state that it is okay if "we talk in secret" about someone else's "strongholds." Please do not mix this up with someone giving counsel. There is a big difference between the two. One avenue of communication is between two people talking about someone else's issues while the other avenue is the person who has an issue speaking to someone they trust, or looking for wisdom from an outsider. We should never abuse our authority by gossiping or "spreading strife among brothers." Your words could lead someone to lose hope and become depressed; that is not part of spreading the good news. Kingdom authority promotes health and well-being to a hurting soul.

> No harm befalls the righteous, But the wicked are filled with trouble.
> Lying lips are an abomination to the LORD, But those who deal faithfully are His delight. A prudent man conceals knowledge, But the heart of fools proclaims folly. (Prov. 12:21–23, NASB)

Again, as we establish our foundation in the realm of authority, we must speak with grace and wisdom. It is important to understand that speaking with authority in the spiritual realm has more of an impact than in the natural. Since the real battle is in the supernatural realm, we must battle from that place of reality to bring change to the earth. We need to remember that what we accomplish in the spirit will affect the natural. We must become acquainted with this reality that we can move in the spirit realm and declare from heaven "it is finished" to that which is causing chaos on the earth.

The flip side is our words and actions in the natural will either propel us into life (i.e., experiencing the blessings of the Lord, encountering His presence, etc.) or death (i.e., experiencing turmoil, sickness, and trial after trial due to the way we speak or the actions we portray).

There is a lot of wisdom we can draw from this above passage (Prov. 12:21–23). Our ability to walk in genuine authority is determined by the words and actions we live by. Christ is the authentic example to follow!

Verse 21 says, "No harm overtakes the righteous, but the wicked have their fill of trouble." Who are the righteous? Anyone who is found in the book of life! Those who have given their heart over to Jesus that He will become their Lord and Savior. As we grow in our relationship with Christ, we must ask the Lord to reveal anything that is wicked in our heart or mind and allow God to minister to those areas.

Having a sinful nature around us will draw us into a place of being deceived, and we begin to believe in the negative words we hear or the ones we speak out. Here is a great prayer I pray: Father, I command my soul to come in line and be submissive to the Holy Spirit. I speak to my spirit man and tell him to align with the movement of God that my words would be full of grace, power and healing that comes from my place of reality, heaven bound in Jesus name, Amen!

If there is any wickedness (disobedience to the precepts found in Christ) within us (i.e., walking in a sinful nature and not repenting and seeking God to deliver us), this becomes a hindrance before Jesus and in return hinders our authority in the spirit. We cannot have blatant disengagement with the Lord and think that we can operate in His authority. The authority we are speaking of is granted through a relationship and trust between us and the Father. Do not let "obvious" sin become a stumbling block in the spirit. The enemy will surround you with thoughts like, "How can you think that you have authority—look at your sin" or "How dare you try to be godly when you have sin in your life?" This is a lie many of us fall into. May we see through the snares of the enemy and believe in who God has called us to be—victorious!

Have you felt that way? Do you ever feel robbed due to the fact that you do not feel worthy of praying for others and, at times, even for yourself? This is a great tactic from the enemy. If he can keep you there, then you are not enforcing the victory of the cross and are not invading his "territory." Today is your day for freedom! Step into the spirit as the beloved of God, having faith to believe that you have been given authority to shift the mountain before you.

I am looking forward to that day when a group of believers step up in faith and go in the spirit, begin to operate in authority as ambassadors of Christ, and disarm the workings of the evil one as they go to meetings that are not opened to the public. Think about it. If the evil one is moving and speaking in these meetings, well, why can't we go in the name of Jesus and do kingdom business and shout the lies down by speaking truth, taking the power of the lying lips, and declaring the love of Jesus over that particular event? If we believe it starts in the spirit realm, well, my golly, we need to get in the spirit and do business!

To be effective in the spirit, we need a heart of repentance as we address any active sin that we are aware of. Speak into the darkness that is surrounding your walk. Call the light of heaven into your life. Command the hands of the enemy off your destiny. Remind him that your God triumphed over him on the cross and believe it! Pray with boldness and understanding that your debt has been cancelled out and that our God disarmed the rulers and authorities! (Col. 2:14–15)

It is your right to release these declarations. It doesn't matter if you have been a Christian for a day or ten years. Make a stand today and declare with authority that the blood of Christ has set you free!

In closing this chapter, I want us to leave with an amazing blessing we see in Proverbs 12:22 (NASB), "Lying lips are an abomination to the LORD, But those who deal faithfully are His delight."

If we keep our words pure and not allow falsehood to have its way in our speech, we are called His delight! In dealing with our tongue, we learn how to walk as His delight. Think about it. You walk into a room of unbelievers, and you have the ability to shine as His delight. In a moment, you step into darkness, but your light shines and clears out the room. Become His delight in all your ways and watch as the room turns and the captives are set free!

Questions

1. Has your tongue been an abomination to the Lord?

2. Have you thought about the three abominations that can be released from your mouth? If they are active in your walk, have you repented?

3. What are your thoughts on Proverbs 12:21–23? How does it apply to your life today?

4. Are you aware of any active sin in your walk today? Have you repented, and are you standing in the power of forgiveness?

5. Will you believe that you can move in the spirit realm and disarm the power of lying lips through Jesus?

6

Battling a Foul Mouth

Do you have a foul mouth? I got ya! Imagine the Lord asking you that question. How would you answer? Some of us would be very quick to say, "No, Lord, for I do not curse." Having a foul mouth is not always speaking some curse word. It is about releasing an offense toward heaven and its will and purposes. If we are to be an example of Christ, then our speech must reflect heaven in all that we say.

Just on a side note, if the leader of the church is moving in the direction given by the Holy Spirit, and you don't agree and begin to question their intentions and speak the opposite, you could be rejecting the purpose of the Lord in that time. Please be careful in what you say or even pray when the Lord shows up in your meetings and things seem out of the ordinary.

> Lying lips are an abomination to the LORD, But those who deal faithfully are His delight. (Prov. 12:22 (NASB)

This verse expresses "lying lips" as an abomination to the Lord. There is no *white lie* before God. Anything that is false is considered a lie. If we have "lying lips," our authority is hindered, for falsehood promotes the intentions of the enemy's camp. If this is active in our lifestyle, it must be resolved immediately! Speaking a lie out is releasing death or a curse into any circumstance. The Lord has no tolerance for a lying mouth, and the church should follow suit!

For an example, how many people do you know who put their trust in the nightly news or what they read on the Internet? If the world can get believers to buy into their lies, they know that it will weaken a man's faith in Jesus. See, the world wants to promote chaos because they have not encountered the love of Jesus, that's where you and I come on the scene to promote truth that dispels the lies. When we experience a personal revival within, then we can become an instrument to birth an awakening around us for the betterment of life itself.

This in not brought up to make us feel condemned but to remind us as we grow in the understanding of keeping our words in line with the integrity defined by the Lord and His Word. That means *stretching the truth* is a lie. If our flesh or the enemy can keep us lying, we are missing out of the blessings of the Lord.

Remember, we are talking about kingdom authority in the spirit. How can we disarm spiritual strong holds if we have "lying lips?" The enemy is prowling the earth to wage war, but as we repent and take authority over his ways, we stop his onslaught. You must be honest with yourself if you are going to move in power and authority. Our words should not be offensive unto the Lord. The enemy hears the words we speak. Do not be fooled. If you have "lying lips" and try to battle a situation without experiencing any freedom, take a step back and ask God to forgive you of your sin. Rebuke the devil and declare that your mouth shall speak the truth in Jesus's name (James 4:7)!

It is our responsibility to gain control of the words we speak. We cannot blame those we are surrounded by. What do I mean? Many years ago, when I was a teenager, I worked on construction sites. Well, let me tell you, almost everyone there had a foul mouth. Every other word would be a curse word. As the days would go by, I would repeat those words in my mind. At times, I found myself repeating lies to fit in with the crowd. (How foolish it was now that I look back— peer pressure is the fear of man that comes from the devil.)

Now I was smart enough not to let these curse words come out while I was home. I had tasted soap, and I did not take a liking to it! So I would say these words in my mind. If someone did something that I did not like, I would curse them out in my mind. I was never big on cursing, but when I did use a foul word, I felt very uneasy. I believe that was the Holy Spirit convicting me because that was not my personality or the standard of my lifestyle.

As I was working one day, having a conversation in my mind, I was cursing someone out because of their stupidity, which made my job harder. At that moment, I realized that

I could turn it on and off anytime I wanted to. Right then, I understood that I could control my thoughts and my words by God's grace. We must get control of our mouth. As a supernatural being, created by a supernatural God, we need to release words of *life* and rebuke the thoughts that do not line up with the heart of the Father.

What is the blessing for those that speak with pure lips?

> But those who deal faithfully are His delight. (Prov. 12:22, NASB)

Those that have a pure mouth are His delight. Wow! What a powerful statement and what a promise we have been given! We need to get this in our walk. It is important to understand that you are His delight. So many believers are walking around with their head hung low, which is a sign of doubt, depression, and a stronghold from the enemy.

This is a great prayer to release daily:

> Father, your word says that I am your delight. Devil, you have no right in my life because I am the beloved. Lord, will you put your words in my mouth. I break the works of the devil off my life and declare that hopelessness, depression, fear, doubt, and anxiety is not from my Father. I command the head of the enemy be crushed in the name of Jesus, amen!

Friends, I want to stress this point: if your heart is for the Lord and you are striving to be right before God but mess up once in a while or find yourself doing something that does not bring God glory, this does not totally negate your ability to move in authority. Remember, we serve a merciful, loving God. Do not let the enemy steal your peace. You are the Lord's delight! Stand from that position, for you are called to live a victorious life. Genuine authority is found and exercised through a lifestyle in the spirit that births encounters with the Most High God. Yes, you may have trials to deal with, but the difference is how you address them. Take the high road. The more time we spend in worship, the more we will notice a change in the way we speak.

Let's Not Be a Fool

Here is another scheme from the enemy. At times, this could be from your peers or those you are close to. The enemy will use anyone who gives an opening to his ways. Have you ever been made fun of, fooled by someone in a way that made you feel unwanted or unaccepted and upset your emotional state? Anyone who will take a stand and voice their authority through Christ will have to battle with someone else's perception of who you are and what you are trying to accomplish for the kingdom. Your mouth is a gateway to either blessings (life) or discouragement (death).

There are bullies even in the church society. We do not need to put up with such actions of selfishness. Many times, they try to bully a person with words that they know will trigger fear, hurt, or depression. Granted, I don't believe everyone that is under this influence may realize it or even wants to walk in it as being the beloved. We need leaders and those in the pew to stand up with a mighty backbone and address this behavior. People come to church to get away from the enemy, not to find him sitting next to them in a service.

Begin to release love over them and their words. As we release love, it begins to expose the root of the curse within that hurting soul. We must understand they are speaking from a place of hurt, mistrust, or being influenced by the enemy. Perfect love casts out all fear. Fear is directing their words, but love destroys fear!

Growing in Stature

A prudent man conceals knowledge, but the heart of fools proclaims folly.

—Proverbs 12:23 (NASB)

If you find yourself being tricked by the enemy through other people or in your own immaturity, you may end up speaking foolishly (i.e., speaking things that the Lord did not share, but stressed such words). Never confess "thus says the Lord" if He really didn't say it! This is a great way to lose credibility and diminish your authority if it truly wasn't the Lord, just words released from your flesh. Be careful ministering such things and finishing with "in the name of Jesus." As we walk through our journey here on earth, I think we could sum up this area of life with this statement: you are remembered by the words you speak and the actions you take. Would you agree?

Think about someone you look up to. There are usually two attributes you are attracted to. First, there is their speech (i.e., the ability to gain your attention and captivate your mind) and the wisdom or knowledge they share. Second would be their actions, how they handle situations and their ability to stay calm during the storms of chaos.

Think about your track record. What do you think you are known for? Are you sharing insightful thoughts or proclaiming folly? The reason we are talking about this issue is if you want to see power and authority in your walk, how does God view your conduct, and, second, how are you viewed among your peers? Are your words likened to a clanging cymbal or words of life and power that brings heavens resources to earth?

> And Jesus increased in wisdom (in broad and full understanding) and in stature and years, and in favor with God and man. (Luke 2:52, AMP)

As you grow in the wisdom and knowledge of God, your stature increases! You begin to gain favor with God and then with man. It is so easy to strive to gain the favor of man because we want to be accepted instantly. To grow in the favor of God is contingent on our faithfulness, purity, integrity, the love we have for others, and our devotion to Him.

What is stature? The dictionary defines it as "quality or status gained by growth, development, or achievement." How does this apply to kingdom authority? Our growth and development within the understanding of God's principles are major keys to move in authority within the spiritual realm. Remember, this authority we are speaking about is the ability to shatter the strongholds around your life, your peers, and your church or community!

Today I encourage your take a look at your walk with Christ. Are you growing, developing, and strengthening your relationship with the Lord? Are you pressing in to gain wisdom and understanding of His Word? Are you studying the Bible to gain knowledge? Do you have a healthy church life? All these things make way for us to grow in the favor of God, which will lead to having favor with men.

The favor of the Lord is a key to moving in authority within the spiritual realm! I'd rather have the favor of God than of men any day so when I speak, the enemies flee, light shines in the darkness, sickness leaves, blind eyes shall open as we see the hand of the Lord in our midst!

As we wrap up this chapter, my prayer is that you grow in understanding the importance of governing your words. Clearly the Lord is concerned about the words we speak and the actions we take. Do not let your words be an abomination to the Lord. May His words be in your mouth as you proclaim the truth and speak with boldness to your enemy! Remember, authority is not just a position but an extension of heaven operating in your life through your words.

Questions

1. Think about your words, are there any white lies mingled in, even in giving an account of a story to make it sound bigger or better?

2. Does your vocabulary change depending on the crowd of people you are with?

3. Are you speaking and releasing folly—basically junk that does not need to be stated?

4. Think about your view of favor. Are you more concerned with fitting in with man or God? Be honest!

5. What are you doing with the foul words around your life?

7

What Are We Confessing?

In this chapter, we will look at what we are confessing. Either it will release the blessing of the Lord (life) or bring a hindrance (death) in our relationship with others and with Christ Himself. I have met many brothers and sisters in the Lord who are just beating themselves up with their own words. If you use the following statements, it is time for a positive change in your life.

Negative Confessions

1. I will never fall in love.
2. My ministry will never take off.
3. I will never be able to do that.
4. Everyone hates me for who I am.
5. I will never find the right person to marry.
6. I will never be as godly as so and so.
7. I have to deal with this sickness.

8. I am stupid and dumb—not worthy.

9. I will always live in poverty.

10. My children will not become anything in this life.

Do you see my point? Our confessions/declarations are the words that surround our mind and penetrate our heart. *Confess negative things, and you will stay negative!* We must confess from a place of victory, releasing positive confessions over our lives and those around us.

So many people are losing this battle. As we confess negativity, we begin to believe those words. We must rise and break every deception that we are confessing. Confess that you are loved! You are loved by the one that created love. Confess that you are able to do all things through Christ. You have to address that evil spirit that is saying you are stupid and not worthy. Speak against the deaf and dumb spirit as Jesus did (Mark 9:25). We need to confess that we are prosperous in Christ and full of potential abiding in His grace. The Bible says, "The righteous shall live off the wealth of the wicked" (Prov. 13:22, NIV). Our best confessions are found in His Word. Open up the Bible and begin to declare His goodness over yourself!

If you are in poverty, confess that the Lord is your provider. Please stop confessing that "this is my life." Rise above the substandard and prepare the way of your future with your confession and faith in Jesus and His promises. (Take some time and search out the promises that have been given to you.) Poverty is not what God has intended. Seek the Lord. Many times we are struggling, and it could be rooted from sin that we entertained. If the enemy can keep us in the dark, then we will continue to confess negativity and not the will of the Lord!

> Those who guard their lips preserve their lives, but those who speak rashly will come to ruin. (Prov. 13:3, NIV)

As we touched on earlier, it is so imperative to guard our lips. Our confession should be in line with the will and purposes of God. We have the authority to break the yokes of the enemy. We cannot serve two masters; our confession will either promote the kingdom of God, or it will give credit to the enemy's camp.

As we meditate on that last statement—our confession will either promote the kingdom of God, or it will give credit to the enemy's camp—some may take an offense. The bottom line is, Are you confessing life or death? Where is your confession derived from? Is it from the will of the Lord? If so, your confession will be positive, even in the midst of the trial you are facing. Or is your confession negative, not from the Lord? It will either be birthed from within our spirit or from the activity of the enemy around us.

The passage above sets the atmosphere for our confession. It is clear we need to watch what we are confessing. We see in this verse that to enjoy life, we must preserve our lips. The meaning of *preserve* is "to put a guard around." We need to get this into our spirit! Take a stand today and confess that the Lord is the protector of your home, family, health, and so on. Spiritual and natural growth is lost because we don't stand up in wisdom and promote kingdom authority.

It's not just that you stand up and release a prayer. It's the faith in the prayer you released and the faith in Jesus to perform that which lines up with His will. Many Christians pray, but so many only get into prayer once the mess comes to their doorstep. I want to see the body in prayer *before* it comes and command it away for this place. Prayer and authority are not meant to only be used when the enemy shows up, but it is meant to be a part of our standard and daily lifestyle.

We must confess words of life on a daily basis; it should be in our spiritual lifestyle. It's a must for all believers. Most confessions will to take place in the face of our enemy. This is exercising our authority in Christ. Yes, Jesus won the victory on the cross. Amen! It is up us to enforce His victory , which we now share, and proclaim, "For me and my house will be a house of prayer." Stop confessing the lies the enemy is speaking into your ear!

The flip side of this passage is, "But those who speak rashly will come to ruin." Again, we are talking about releasing life or death through our words. This passage is clear on the result we will have if we do not control our tongue. Someone speaking rashly does not think about what they are saying, nor cares about what ramifications could be upon them or the one they are speaking to. The Bible is clear on this. If we speak negative things over others, we will also pay the consequence. Be careful and do not fall into this snare!

Positive Confessions

There are a lot of teachings among the Christian community about positive confessions. This journey is not about the "claim it" confessions. Meaning, you see a Cadillac that you like, so you claim it in Jesus's name. Let's journey down the path of releasing words that are soothing to the soul, whether it would be over you or someone else. A positive confession is being wise with the words you choose to use. The main goal is to gain peace and spiritual land that over takes the natural realm. It's not about gaining materialistic things but controlling the level of peace in your atmosphere.

> A gentle tongue [with its healing power] is a tree of life, but willful contrariness in it breaks down the spirit. (Prov. 15:4, AMP)

I love this verse! It is soothing to just read it. If we are striving to minister with genuine authority, it must be based in love. When we look at the teachings of Jesus, the end result was to always express the Father's love for them so they would see the goodness of God. Even when He had to correct them, it was out of love.

May we be known for having a *gentle* tongue in all aspects of life, whether we are speaking to our mate, children, friends, family, clients, employees, or a stranger. I pray that our words will always be positive to the one we are speaking to. At times, they may seem harsh. True love and genuine authority creates boundaries between two people. This is a growing goal within me every day, that I will have a spiritual balance in my walk and exercise authority in a right matter before the Lord. Be wise in who you allow into the matters of your heart. For me, only those that I know that speak in love, wisdom, and from the perspective of heaven have the right to speak into such matters with in my life.

One translation says, "A soothing tongue is a tree of life." What does *soothing* mean?

> Having a calming, assuaging, or relieving effect–restoring confidence and relieving anxiety; a very reassuring remark.

What a great picture the Lord has given us. This passage is another block we must have in our foundation to move in authentic authority that releases hope to people and growth to our land.

Our words should bring life to someone that is suffering. Say Bettie just received word from her doctor that she has an illness. What do we confess? Do we align our faith and confession with the doctor's diagnosis? No, we align our confession with what the Word of the Lord says about Bettie. We are not neglecting that Bettie has an illness. May we become people who do not entertain the diagnosis but align with the potential reward of the Father's love, which is healing!

I am sure most of you can relate when I say that a diagnosis from a doctor can weigh very heavily on our shoulders. Too many times, that is the place where people stay. They never get to the point of confessing with boldness what the Word says but continue to walk around confessing their diagnosis. I want to challenge you to see past the now and explore by faith the realities of Jesus. This comes by seeking the kingdom first through prayer and worship.

We need to be aware that *no* sickness comes from Jesus. He doesn't make you sick so you can endure in hopes to help another person. Sickness is not from heaven. The result is. Furthermore, sickness is not a thorn in your side planted by the Lord. If He is the healer, why in the world would He make you sick? Doesn't that seem to contradict itself?

There have been many times I would pray for someone who had multiple illnesses and see the Lord heal them instantly, and other times, I would only witness two out of four things touched. We need to leave that in the hands of the Lord but pursue speaking healing over people, whether we see an immediate healing or not. It may take a few times of prayer to see it manifest. Either way, we are invoking the power that comes from heaven through us as we speak in faith, power, and authority.

Remember in the beginning of this book, we spoke about the Lord speaking light into darkness? I explained that there was a need and that God spoke the result. The same is true with our story about Bettie. *We must stop confessing the diagnosis and start proclaiming the results!*

I do not take sickness lightly, nor the fact that there are real health issues that we have to face in this world. But we need to focus on the One that heals! Please do not be ignorant to either the sickness or Jesus the healer, meaning don't get up and throw your medicine away until Jesus tells you to or you have a supernatural encounter that heals your sickness, which He loves to do!

At lunch one day, I took a walk at the local park. I was experiencing some pain in my knee. I thought, *Jesus is my healer, He is in heaven, and I am able to go in the spirit where He is, per John 10.*

At that point, I said a prayer that went something like this: "Father, by faith I step into heaven as Jesus is my door [access point] to come before my healer. As I stand in the heavenly realm, I ask for my knee to be healed."

Instantly the pain left. The Father was teaching me to go into His presence not just by thinking about it but by actually applying faith that allowed me to enter to receive and not just stand far off and cry out for my healing.

Take some time and read and pray through Hebrews 4:16 (Mirror Translation), "For this reason we can approach the authoritative throne of grace with bold utterance. We are welcome there in His embrace, and are reinforced with immediate effect in times of trouble."

Questions

1. Are you releasing negative confessions?

2. What are some of the positive confessions you released today?

3. Do you speak rashly to others at a situation you are dealing with?

4. Are you confessing the diagnosis or the result?

5. Do you believe Jesus is still at work today healing people?

8

Who Has Authority

Who has been given the ability to exercise kingdom authority found in the name of Jesus today? A better question is, Are you walking in your God-given authority? Looking across the church society, many believers leave this area up to their pastor or the leaders of the church. That mind-set does not line up with the Bible in any way. Many are walking around confessing a lie, which would sound something like this: "I am not able to do that because I am not ordained or have a leadership position."

May we find grace and freedom in 2 Corinthians 3:2 (Mirror Translation), "Instead of an impressive certificate framed on my wall I have you framed in my heart." There is nothing wrong with those who study and receive a certificate, I am all for it, but let's not let that determine who can walk and promote true kingdom authority. It's what's in the heart and the relationship we have with Jesus that determines the level of authority we will walk in.

Have you ever felt that way? Maybe you find yourself thinking, *Well, only the leadership team can preach the Gospel, heal the sick, cast out demons, and raise the dead.* What a misunderstanding of the Scripture and a snare we can fall into. Just think about the pressure and expectancy we put on those men and women in leadership. May we be people who do not set up our leaders to fail or put them on a pedestal. Become supportive in your prayer life for those who are leading the church you attend and be confident in who the Lord has created you to be and the place of influence you walk in.

Can we agree that we are called to be a disciple of Christ?

> And when he had found him, he brought him back to Antioch. For a whole year they assembled together with and were guests of the church and instructed a large number of people; and in Antioch the disciples were first called Christians. (Acts 11:26, NASB)

The disciples were called Christians. Anyone following the principles of Christ and call Him Lord and Savior of their life is a Christian and has the right to move in His authority.

In Matthew 10, we see the authority Jesus gave to the first disciples and applies to His disciples today, which is you and I!

> Jesus called his twelve disciples to him and gave them authority to drive out impure spirits and to heal every disease and sickness. (Matt. 10:1, NIV)

These twelve Jesus sent out with the following instructions: "Do not go among the Gentiles or enter any town of the Samaritans. Go rather to the lost sheep of Israel. As you go, proclaim this message: 'The kingdom of heaven has come near.' Heal the sick, raise the dead, cleanse those who have leprosy, drive out demons. Freely you have received; freely give. (Matt. 10:5–8, NIV)

Here are a few comparisons between the disciples of yesterday and of those today. It is important to get this into your spirit!

1. These men spent time within the presence of Jesus. We must have a daily interactive relationship with Christ.

2. These men spent time in prayer with Jesus. We must have a daily prayer life.

3. These men presented questions to Jesus. If we do not understand something, we must seek it out in prayer and through our daily devotion of the Word.

4. There was nothing special with these men, but they answered the call. The same is said for us today. We must not put anyone on a pedestal but be who God called us to be!

5. These men did not have a total understanding of the anointing found in the Holy Spirit right away.

The same goes for us today. We must press in, and the Lord will reveal Himself through us daily as we commune with the Holy Spirit.

This list could go on and on. My point is this: they were just like us (but they were willing to follow at any cost). They answered the call, just like you and me! In doing so, Christ has given us His authority to move spiritual mountains. Do not let the enemy hold that lie over you any longer. Confess that you are free through the name of Jesus! You have answered the call and will move in the anointing of Holy Spirit and destroy the yokes of the enemy! Allow the supernatural power to flow through your life and expect marvelous things to happen so His glory will be known!

You may not feel any different, but your confession has changed, and you will become awakened in the Spirit. We must realize that we are all called to operate in His authority to spread the Gospel, heal the sick, cast out demons, and raise the dead. Release this over your life: In the name of Jesus, I will share the Gospel. I will lay hands on the sick, and they shall be healed. I will move in discernment and cast out every demon that raises its head, and by the Holy Spirit, I shall raise the dead!

As we do this, we are aligning our faith, hope, and spirit to the authority we have been given as a disciple of Christ. It is imperative to understand the meaning of authority we find in Matthew 10:1. The word is *exousia. It is permissible, allowed, right, liberty, power to do anything.*

Basically the Lord is saying that you have the right and liberty to enforce his authority. In doing so, you have the ability to speak the Gospel and heal the sick. You have power over any demon and the right to raise the dead as He sees fit! Take a moment and think about those words. *You* have the right, the power, and the permission to represent His authority on earth and in the spirit realm. *You* have the power to do *anything* through His name that aligns with His will. It does not say, "Only pastors, elders, deacons, or leaders have the right." *You* have the right!

In your own words, release a prayer along these lines: Father, forgive me for not taking my place in the spirit. I pray that you will release your wisdom to me to move in this realm of authority. I want to spread the Gospel, heal the sick, cast out demons, and raise the dead through your name. Father, I command the hands of the devil off my life, my mind, and my spirit. Help me to walk in faith in the spirit to enforce what is mine. I break every word that has been spoken over me that is not of the Lord, and I bind my mind to the mind of Christ.

We must understand that authority is not just a position someone walks in. It is someone who *aligns* their faith, devotion, and trust with the *One* that issues such authority. As we learn how to align our faith, confessions, and attitude with the will and purposes of God, He will reveal His spirit in a way that will take us further in the supernatural.

God has not created us to be like *robots*, where we have no understanding. He created us in a way that we shall colabor with Him and *understand* His authority. Have you ever heard the term *yes-man*? Meaning someone who just says yes to make his "leader" happy with his ways and actions? This in not the relationship Christ is looking for. Nor will it give you the ability to move in the spirit. God knows what is in the heart of a man no matter what his mouth may be confessing. We cannot just say yes with no action taken. It would be like someone giving you a new car, but you never drive it. His authority was given to us for a reason—to be enforced from the spirit to the natural realm!

One purpose of this book is to get your mind thinking in a new direction or to refresh things that you may have heard but may have walked away from. We may never understand the total depth of His authority because He is God, but we are able to gain and walk in a place of authority to govern the spiritual realm around our family, home, job, church, and community!

Imagine what a service would be like if a group of people acted on their position in the spirit and spoke with faith over their land? It would not be the typical meeting, but what we are experiencing in our Sunday meetings, or even our midweek gatherings, the typical picture of what the Lord thinks the meetings should be like?

I was in a service on November 22, 2015 (Living Springs Global Fellowship), with some other believers who knew their rightful place in the spirit. In that time, the Lord took us in the spirit to the Middle East to speak over an oil field to stop the attack from ISIS in taking oil. I believe this was a response to a warning in the spirit realm, and we reacted to the call. (*I mean, who thinks about going to the Middle East during worship, let alone addressing the spirit behind a movement like ISIS.*) I could feel the sand hitting my face as I stood in faith declaring protection over the oil field, and I asked the Lord to release angels to stand on guard against the attack of the enemy. This was a day doing our part in the spirit of the Lord!

The next day, I had an impression to review the news to see if there was anything being said about oil fields and ISIS in the Middle East. There it was. The headline read, "US Strike Destroys Hundreds of ISIS Oil Tankers in Syria." I share this to build faith in us to go out and believe for more than what we see before us. We really can make a change and see our culture transform as it starts in the spirit and manifests in the natural!

> I have given you authority to trample on snakes and scorpions and to overcome all the power of the enemy; nothing will harm you. However, do not rejoice that the spirits submit to you, but rejoice that your names are written in heaven. (Luke 10:19–20, NIV)

This is another passage wherein we see the Lord releasing His authority, this time to the seventy He sent out. It is imperative that we submit to verse 20, "However, do not rejoice that the spirits submit to you, but rejoice that your name is written in heaven." Never let your emotional excitement get before your humility. It is valuable to know that we have this authority to beat our enemy at his game, but we must always stay humble and rejoice that our name is written in heaven!

Again, anyone who calls on Jesus as their Savior is entitled to walk in authority by spreading the Gospel, healing the sick, casting out demons, and raising the dead. I have experienced the first three actions many times in my ministry. I believe one day the Lord will use me to raise the dead as He sees fit!

Many years ago, a dear friend of mine passed away in a car accident. When I heard the news, I went right into prayer. There were many of us praying. I heard the Lord in this time, "Go to the hospital and lie on his body and speak life into his soul." I did not do that. I fell into fear and decided to just pray from home. We do not always know the plan of the Lord, but we should have the attitude of, "Yes, Lord, here I am. Send me!"

There I was trying to pray with authority, calling my friend back to life as I prayed for hours. As the days went by, I began to think about how I *sidestepped* the Word of the Lord. If we are going to walk in this authority, we must follow whatever the Lord speaks to us. Reacting to His Word with disobedience misaligns us with His purpose. It will align us with the plans of the enemy. Did my friend go to heaven too soon because of my disobedience? I hope that is not the case. (*We serve a merciful God.*) Did I walk in the full power of Christ at that time? No, due to the fact that I disobeyed in what I heard the Lord spoke to me.

I believe the Lord will test us to see if we will be obedient. To declare and see His authority manifest, we must obey His commands. My point to this story is not about the Lord raising my friend from the dead but about my lack of obedience. It is nothing for the Lord to raise the dead, but we must choose to obey no matter what the cost may be!

Many times, we confess, "Yes, Lord" while things are going well, but in the midst of a trial, we may confess one thing and walk in the opposite direction. Let's use my story. I prayed numerous times before that accident to hear from God and that I would be used to spread the Gospel, heal the sick, cast out demons, and raise the dead. Prayers like, "Send me anywhere Lord, and I will obey!" At the time of the accident, my *words* were *yes*, but my actions were *no* because I gave in to the snares of the enemy. (*Remember that there is no condemnation for those who are in Christ.*)

My point is, to walk in authority to the fullest, we must be obedient to the written *and* spoken Word of God. To gain recognition in the spirit by the Lord and the enemy, we must to be aligned with Christ in spirit, soul, and mind.

9

Authority over Our Children

Let's take an adventure down a road I like to call "household chaos." Do you ever feel stress or tension in your home, maybe between you and your spouse or with your children? How about those lovely houseguests? In one of His parables, Jesus made this statement found in the book of Mark.

> And if a house is divided (split into factions and rebelling) against itself, that house will not be able to last. (Mark 3:20–30, AMP)

You may have experienced this or may find yourself in the midst of this taking place in your home today. What could bring division into a home? Many times there is a lot of *finger pointing* that goes along with division. Too often, our human nature wants to put the blame on someone else so we do not feel guilty or have to pay the consequence for our actions. Today we must begin to refocus our thoughts and prayer life so we can take back our home!

There are many Christians that deal with arguing in their homes, and it is chalked up to being *normal*. Yes, Christians do yell at each other. Why is that? Why do Christians battle with each other? Why do Christians give others an attitude? First and foremost, we are not perfect *yet*; we are a work in progress. With that being said, I have heard too many Christians use that as an excuse for their actions. I would like be the first to say that it is not acceptable for me to use that excuse when I have a bad day. *(On a side note, my beautiful wife and I have been married for ten years and suffered two arguments. I mention this to inspire hope as you can have an amazing marriage as Jesus is the center.)*

There are a few things that could be the cause of division in a home. A big issue could be the lack of headship. Some form of positive leadership is needed in every home. Who is the voice of reason that will take the responsibility for their family? As the head of the home, you become the gatekeeper. You determine what is allowed to come in, and you must keep out what is not wanted! Who is watching the gateway of your home? Do you believe you can stand up and stop the enemy before he enters?

There are many broken homes within the Christian community, and we want to be sensitive but also bring an awareness that there needs to be a spiritual leader in the home. In any home that is represented as a *Christian home,* there should be an established spiritual voice of authority. Either the man or the woman, depending on the circumstances, has to take a position in the spirit to be the leader of that home.

Clearly, for all the men reading this, God has called you the leader. Please do not abuse that role. As a married couple, you are to work together and raise your family in wisdom and unison with your mate. There is a lot of control that is being abused when it comes to "headship" within the home. Yes, we as fathers and husbands will be judged for the actions we walk in as "the man of the house," but we should never disrespect our spouse. There should be a healthy communication between each other so we walk as one just as Christ called us to be!

Being the head of your home as Christ is the head of the church, you have a responsibility in the natural and spiritual realm to exercise your authority in Christ. You are to represent Christ in the natural and stand as His ambassador in the spirit. Your words should align with the Gospel. When you speak to family members, there needs to be grace on your words. As you enforce discipline, you must do it in love. I know of many Christian homes that do not enforce discipline on a regular basis, which causes a problem when things get out of hand. A lack of love creates an atmosphere for arguments.

Many parents are struggling to have control over the way their children speak to them. It is our duty as a parent and leader of the home to harness the words that are spoken to each other. How is that accomplished? Here are four basic principles you could apply in your home.

1.   Intercession over your family members

2. Daily devotion in the home

3. Leading by example in speech and actions.

4. Using positive reinforcement while speaking to them, especially in regard to discipline

It is important to understand that the way we speak to our children will affect them as they grow and find their own personality. Are you uplifting your child on a daily basis? Think about the words you use when they make a mistake or get into trouble? How do you address the situation?

As parents, and being the authority figure over our children, if we do not speak wisdom, knowledge, love, and direction, the world will gain their attention. We must, at all costs, take ownership of our children. It is our right to speak over them in the spirit. If we do not do this, the enemy will be able to win them over. As a parent, we have been given a priceless gift. Let's not lose them because of a lack of understanding or not standing in the gap. With that being said, they still have a will and ability to make bad decisions. It is our goal to love them through it.

Maybe some of you are asking, How do I accomplish this? What do we say or pray to protect our children? Let me be clear. We cannot forcefully change someone's will. God is not about manipulation, but He is in the business of showing love! If we do not pray, it is like going into battle and leaving our weapons behind, and we will be defeated.

For we are God's [own] handiwork [His workmanship], recreated in Christ Jesus, [born anew] that we may do those good works which God predestined [planned beforehand] for us [taking paths which He prepared ahead of time], that we should walk in them [living the good life which He prearranged and made ready for us to live]. (Eph. 2:10, AMP)

How do we use this verse in prayer for our children? Let's break it down:

1. "For we are God's [own] handiwork [His workmanship], recreated in Christ Jesus, [born anew]"—If your child is not following Jesus, call them by name into the light. Speak to the darkness that is surrounding them. It is your right to do so! *If you do not call them, who will?* If you do not speak life over them, what difference do they know? If you do not take authority in the spirit, your enemy will gain a stronghold in their soul.

2. "That we may do those good works which God predestined [planned beforehand]"—Have you prayed to find out what plans the Lord has for your child? Have you spoken destiny over their walk? Take a look at their words. Is it birthing life or death? If the Lord has revealed their calling, are you praying that into being? God has a plan for all of us. Use your authority to speak to their potential!

3. "Taking paths which He prepared ahead of time, that we should walk in them"—Bind their feet to walk on the paths that were prepared ahead for them! Call them to walk in the fullness of God. Declare that your child walk the path of righteousness. Ask God to reveal to them these paths. Again this is tied to their calling.

4. "That we should walk in them [living the good life which He prearranged and made ready for us to live]"—Call the blessing of the Lord into their life, even from the day they are born; age does not matter in the spirit. Call that what God has ordained into being (i.e. a good life). God created us to have a good life. We need to enforce that in the spirit realm. Either the enemy or our selfish desires take us off this path.

Speak positive things over your children and see positive results! Yes, they have their own will and might act up at times, but we can govern the spiritual aspect as a parent because God has given us that authority. It doesn't matter at was stage your child is at in their relationship with Christ, we should always speak this over them!

Prayer for My Children

I use this passage in my intercession over my girls. I call their feet to the paths that the Lord has ordained for them to walk on. I speak life to their bodies, that no sickness or disease shall harm them. I call their destiny to be filled to the fullness that God intended it to be! I call their minds to be of the mind of Christ, that they would hear and see the things of God. I ask the Lord to give them visions and dreams all their days, that they would see the purpose of God in their lives.

This is a starting point for you to pray for your children or those that you love. This is the beginning of taking your loved ones back from the darkness. It's not enough to sing songs about going to the enemy's camp. Go there and do kingdom business and wipe it out! Some sing about it and end up there because they did not enforce their authority within their prayer life, nor had faith to believe that their prayers were making a difference.

Take hold of that which is yours! Use wisdom and authority in the Spirit to protect your loved ones. I am sure some of you have the enemy in your ear, saying, "This is for those that give themselves to prayer for hours a day." That is a lie right from hell. Not everyone has the heart for intercession, but we are all called to have a prayer life! We have the right and ability to speak to the spiritual atmosphere over those who are under our spiritual covering.

I would like to tell you today that whatever level of prayer you are walking in, it carries authority from heaven, and you have the power to speak life and death over your loved ones. Remember, who is going to speak into the heart of your children, over your church, home, or work? It will either be words of life or death. Either you will eat the fruit of life or death!

Shelby Awaken at Night

I would like to share this short story to end this chapter. I was writing this portion of the chapter one night while everyone was in bed, and I had some quiet time to myself! So there I was punching away on the keys, and I heard Shelby wake up crying. Now this is not typical for her as she sleeps through the night. I heard my wife go into her room to comfort her. A few moments later, the crying stopped. I was like, "Thank you, Jesus!" Well, I celebrated a little too fast. She started to cry again. This time, I did not hear my wife get out of bed. I took that as, "Les, come upstairs and take care of this."

Well, I did take care of it. As I was walking up the stairs, I heard, "Take a stand on her behalf." So I went in and got her out of the crib. As I held her, I began to pray over her, asking the Lord to reveal what the issue was so I could address it. I began to pray. I took authority over fear and anxiety, breaking the power of any negative dream. Then I called the peace of God over her mind, body, and spirit. I called her body to receive sweet sleep from the Lord.

Now I did not know what the issue was exactly, but that was the prayer I released. I could have gone in there and rocked her to see if she would fall asleep, but we have authority. Let's use it! If we cancel out a negative motive, please be sure to fill it with a positive word from the Lord, meaning if you cancel out death, make sure to fill it with life.

Questions

1. What are your thoughts and ideas of what headship should look like in your home?

2. What words do you use when your child or someone acts up and does wrong?

3. Are you praying, asking the Lord to reveal His will and purposes for your child?

4. Have you asked for forgiveness from a loved one if you have reacted wrongly to a problem?

5. Have you prayed Ephesians 2:10 over your loved ones today?

10

Authority over Our Community

As you drive through your community, do you notice how many bars, nightclubs, psychic readers, gang hangouts, school drug free zone, hospitals, and other "specialty" treatment centers are located within your township? This chapter is about enforcing our authority in the spirit over the demonic activity that has taken over many cities today.

Our Home

Wherever we live, that is the land the Lord has given us. It is our duty to call the presence of the Lord into our communities. If we are not exercising spiritual authority in our land, who do you think will control your community?

> For if you diligently keep all this commandment which I command you to do, to love the Lord your God, to walk in all His ways, and to cleave to Him—Then the Lord will drive out all these nations before you, and you shall dispossess nations greater and mightier than you. Every place upon which the sole of your foot shall tread shall be yours: from the wilderness to

> Lebanon, and from the River, the river Euphrates, to the western sea [the Mediterranean] your territory shall be. There shall no man be able to stand before you; the Lord your God shall lay the fear and the dread of you upon all the land that you shall tread, as He has said to you. (Deut. 11:22–25, AMP)

Many years ago, the Lord spoke to me about verse 24, "Every place upon which the sole of your foot shall tread shall be yours." The question today is, How open will we be in regard to the spiritual realm? We need to understand that it is as real and tangible as those things that we see and feel in the natural. As we gain understanding that we are in a battle, we have the authority to speak over the works of our enemy. He wants to destroy us. God had provided the victory so we may succeed in the land we find ourselves standing in.

Let's focus on the home you are living in. Many of us may not know the history behind the home we are renting or have purchased. We do not know what may have happened on the land the home was built on. When my wife and I bought our home, the first day, we took ownership, I walked the property and called the blessing of the Lord to be evident all the days that we lived there. As we walked through the home, I prayed for a cleansing to take place in the spirit. I rebuked all activity that was not of the Lord that had taken place on my new land and asked for His angels to have charge over my home.

If we are going to move in authority, we must understand that the enemy will try to derail us or, at best, hinder us from walking in the power and authority we have in God. Do not give into his lies; take ownership of your land. If the previous owners were not Christians, it would be obvious that the home needs to be committed to Christ. If it was owned by a Christian, we do not know what may have been done in secret.

This principle is the same for anyone buying a new home. We do not know what spiritual residue the builders left behind or if there was any spiritual activity done from unwanted "guests" at the time the home was being built. It is your home. As you take ownership in the natural, please take ownership in the spirit.

Your prayer could be something like this: Father, in the name of Jesus, I commit this home and land to your will. I ask that your purpose will be fulfilled in my home. I command all activity of the devil to stop in the name of Jesus. I ask that you release your judgment on those actions. Father, I command this home to be full of your peace. I rebuke and take authority over all negativity that has been in this home. I destroy the works of sickness, depression, anger, and hopelessness (and whatever the Lord may speak) that has been upon this land. Have your way in this home and I ask that your joy, health and blessings will be released here today.

If you see anything negative rise up in your home, you need to address it immediately. We do not want to give the enemy any room to stand on. We should control the activity in our home, not the enemy. Just as we invest in the natural by paying our mortgage, the same is true in the spirit; invest into your home through your intercession!

Every time I do yard work, I speak over my home and remind the Lord that I have committed it unto Him for His use. I ask the Lord to release angels to minister the good intentions of heaven toward those that step onto my land and that they would have an encounter with the Holy Spirit. I want my home to be different than those around me, as I pursue to love righteousness and hate wickedness, that I would be set apart from my companions (see Heb. 1:9).

One day as a friend was driving down my road, he saw a bright beam of light going from my roof to the sky, like a portal. I have experienced this firsthand numerous times as I witnessed the activity of angels in my home and the ministry of the Holy Spirit to many who have come to fellowship with my family. Yes, my prayers invoked heaven, and because of this, we experience Jesus's presence tangibly whenever we labor with him. So can you. Start asking today!

Our Community

Most communities today will have some type of municipal complex where a group of men and women *control* certain activities that are allowed to go on within that town. Some of those boards will control planning/zoning laws, taxes, building codes, and so on. They have the *voice of authority* over your community. Within my community, if I want to build on my land, I have to go before the board to get it approved, even though it is my land.

Think about how our communities would be healthier and stronger and have more balance in both the spirit and natural realm if the local church would rise and have a "spiritual board"—men and women who would gather to seek the Lord to move through their town, to pray and tear down the strongholds that are infiltrating their land. Imagine a group of believers standing up to enforce biblical authority in the land—and not just on a Sunday morning.

I am not speaking about a prayer meeting to just gather people but one that moves in purpose and power, exposing darkness and making a stand before God and man, a prayer meeting that gets a reputation that things get done when they gather in the name of Jesus. It would be attended by a group of people who go past the traditional prayers offered up and engage heaven to do kingdom business for those around them, a group that shakes apathy and not stand for second-rate lifestyles any longer, a group that has visitations with Jesus and whose steps are directed by Him. This group would have an effect on the spiritual landscape of their community. I would always go to that meeting!

The church that I grew up in was led by a great man who had a heart of prayer (thank you, Pastor Wes Newell). It was obvious that we had a praying church, and not just for the congregation. We had all-night prayer meetings every month for some time. The goal was to gather people and intercede over our communities to hear what the will and purposes of the Lord was for our land. We would have a map of South Jersey and pray over each county as we waited on the Lord for direction. There were many great nights of prayer, and we saw numerous prayers answered!

One of our targets was a local beach that was dedicated as a nudist destination. This did not sit well with our spirits, nor was it attractive. We gathered on different occasions to pray and call the hand of the Lord on that beach. Some of us walked the beach at night and asked for forgiveness for the sins committed and for the Lord to restore the true beauty of this beach. Today, it is no longer a nudist beach through the name of Jesus! Yes, our prayers were answered. Stand strong, beloved, for yours should come to pass also.

Restoring a Barren Land

> For I will pour water upon him who is thirsty, and floods upon the dry ground. I will pour My Spirit upon your offspring, and My blessing upon your descendants. And they shall spring up among the grass like willows or poplars by the watercourses. (Isa. 44:3–4, AMP)

This passage is a mighty reference for prayer over our communities. We must take a stand! We must join with the church family in our communities, asking the Lord to open up the heavens and rain down upon our dry land, that revival breaks out within the church that will lead to souls being committed to the kingdom of God.

Imagine different denominations coming together to pray for a movement of God in your community. Do what it takes to gather people in your church and pray with authority. Shatter the walls that are between you and other churches. It doesn't matter what church erected them. We must spiritually demolish them in the name of Jesus. Pray for the hearts of the leaders who represent each church. Let's go further and call the saints who are in the pews to be awakened in the spirit so they will take their place in His river and be influential wherever they go. May we see supernatural manifestations of His love, power, miracles, healing, and salvation and may they be an everyday occurrence in our land!

One of the biggest issues in this area is the negativity that is being released within the church today, meaning there is a lot of *slandering* that goes on among church people regarding denominational indifferences. Speaking against another denomination is like speaking death to God's will and your extended family. Where is it stated that there should be ten different denominations represented in a community? (*He is looking for one church with one voice that may meet in different locations.*)

It is time that we take a stand in the gap before God for our community. It's not about an "evangelist outreach" to get more people in our pews. No, we need to call the will of the Lord into our land to destroy the works of the enemy. Its not about Sunday morning. It's about where people are on Tuesday afternoon. Are they feeling the love of God or being tormented by the enemy?

Let's go back to the passage above. Cry out in intercession for God to pour out His water in your land. Call His spirit into the dry areas. What are these dry areas? The bars, gentlemen clubs, hospitals, drug and gang areas, areas where the psychic readers are doing their evil work, and so on—any place that does not bring glory to God.

Begin to use what you have been given. Declare and command those works to be destroyed. Now let's make it clear, we are not asking for ill will to come upon the people involved. No, we are asking that the Holy Spirit will convict them of their sins. Do not judge them but take a stand toward their actions in the spirit and cast down righteous judgment upon the works of the enemy, not on the person!

If we do not stand up for our communities in prayer, what gives us the right to complain about the evil works going on? It is like complaining about our president, but you do not cast a vote, which represents your voice on the determination of who gets elected. There is a lot of complaining and not enough prayer being lifted up. We put our noses up toward the "sinners" in our land but will not take an hour and lift them up in prayer. Doesn't that seem backward and misaligned with the Word? If we are going to win our community back, it must start in prayer and finish in worship!

Drive by Intercession

As you drive within the limits of your community, begin to call the blessing of the Lord upon those who are not *yet* in the kingdom. Pray that a spirit of repentance would fall in the land, that men and women, young and old, would get saved! When you see people at the bus stop, speak the blessing of life over them. Pray that the hand of the Lord would move upon them and His will and purposes be known. If you see a drug deal going on, stop cursing them with your mouth and start speaking life over them! Whatever sin we see within our land, we must stop speaking death and start releasing life into the situation.

Let's say you see someone going into a bar. He may be an alcoholic. Instead of thinking, *There goes the town's alcoholic*, call his soul to feel the love of Christ. Ask the Lord to release His kindness on that person. Pray for salvation to flood his soul. Speak life over him. Stop cursing him with your words. The world sees him as an alcoholic, but God sees him as one of His lost children. Think about what you speak over your community and ask God for a revelation on how He sees your land.

As believers, we can spiritually govern what goes on in our land. It is just as important to address the issues in the spirit as it is to walk and act true to our confession of love for Christ in the natural. There needs to be repentance for those words and actions done in our communities that do not bring Gods glory on the scene. Who will set the example?

> If my people, who are called by my name, will humble themselves and pray and seek my face and turn from their wicked ways, then I will hear from heaven, and I will forgive their sin and will heal their land. Now my eyes will be open and my ears attentive to the prayers offered in this place. (2 Chron. 7:14–15, NIV)

We are talking about our words having an impact on our communities. It is important to stop cursing our land and start proclaiming that God's will be fulfilled. The above passage shows us we must have a heart that is willing to repent so God will hear our prayers, meaning it is not okay to say negative things about what is going on in your community and to think that if you pray, God will move. *We can not confess negativity and expect positive results.* No, we must be aware of the words we are releasing, and if we speak death, we must repent so our prayers will not be hindered.

I love the second part—"and I will forgive their sin and will heal their land." Our repentance and the way that we change our declarations over our community will align us to receive God's promise. If we repent and govern what we say, God has to move and heal our land. He is a faithful Father that fulfills His promises! To heal our land can range from doing away with crime and abuse to physically touching the land so it can harvest vegetation once again. It is a healing both spiritually and physically.

To close, I will share a short testimony about one move of God I was able to witness in my community. As I was driving to work one day, I went by a building where a psychic reader performed their ritual. As I went by, I heard the Lord say, "Take that land back." Every day for a few years, I would pray as I drove by, "Lord, I take authority over that land and curse the works of the devil and command that work to be shut down in Jesus's name." Today that place sits in ruin. I believe God moved and the enemy lost his place.

I did not speak negativity over the person who was operating there but took offense toward the enemy for setting up camp in my land. This is one way to exercise our authority and govern the spiritual activity that is taking place in our land. I do want to point out, this is not a game. Please do not take this lightly; as we walk in authority, we must keep our walk straight before the Lord. Be led by the spirit and use wisdom in those spiritual endeavors you will embark upon! *Do not arouse the enemy if you are not willing*

11

Authority within the Church

> Brothers and sisters, I could not address you as people who live by the Spirit but as people who are still worldly—mere infants in Christ. I gave you milk, not solid food, for you were not yet ready for it. Indeed, you are still not ready. You are still worldly. For since there is jealousy and quarreling among you, are you not worldly? Are you not acting like mere humans? (1 Cor. 3:1–3, NIV)

As I prayed to figure out how to start this chapter, my spirit was drawn to this passage. I need to be obedient to the Lord and share what is in my spirit. This chapter may be *touchy* for some of us because we will address some real issues regarding speaking *life and death* within the fours walls of our church.

Reading Paul's letter to the Corinthian church, there were problems back then just as there are today. There is a lot of misunderstanding and hurt that goes on within the church, and much of it is caused by our words and the actions we portray. It is sad and a disgrace to see the enemy having his way in our churches. This is supposed to be our land, a place to gather to worship, learn, and fellowship with the Lord's family, and in many areas, it has been given over to the enemy. We need to wake up, beloved, and put a stop to the ways of the enemy that is causing division in the house of God.

> You are still worldly. For since there is jealousy and quarreling among you, are you not worldly? Are you not acting like mere humans?

What do we see in this passage? If you remember, in the beginning of this book, we talked about positive and or negative authority coming in two basic forms—speech and action. Jealousy is an emotional/physical action. Quarreling leads to an action of death. How can we destroy the works of the enemy in our camp if we have negative words and actions taking place?

One example we can find within the last few years has been in regard to the *style* of worship. Many churches have decided to do a *traditional* and a *contemporary* service. Think about the negativity that has been released. The church has allowed lyrics and the sound of the instruments to bring division among the people. I know this could be a sore spot, but we have to be honest before God. Division is a separation, correct? Men and women who are in leadership have given way to those that are complaining about worship. The complaining has undermined the authority of the church and created division. The church has come to a point of division so the pews stay full. *(I don't want you to think that I am hardened when it comes to meeting someone's needs, but meeting a need should not bring division among the body of believers.)*

Negative words have been spoken by the worship team and those in the pew about each other and toward the leaders, and it has to stop if we are going to be a healthy church. We are to come together as one and worship in unity! It is time to put away our childish behavior and become men and women with one heart and one vision—to bless the Lord and reach the lost.

If we have backbiting, gossip, slander, and quarrelling in the church, how is that going to win the lost? They are coming in to get away from that mess, and yet we allow it to go on in so many ways. Think about your words, what you have said in the past or even today. Are your words building up or tearing down your church body? Are you speaking negativity because you do not like something the pastor has said or because they have implemented some type of change within the church?

Talking about the pastor or leadership team (or anyone) behind their back is slander, and the enemy will thrive on this action. The meaning of *slander* is "oral communication of false statements injurious to a person's reputation, A false and malicious statement or report about someone."

If you have participated in causing any quarrelling among those in your church, please repent and take ownership of your words today.

Loyalty to Our Church Leaders

> Have confidence in your leaders and submit to their authority, because they keep watch over you as those who must give an account. Do this so that their work will be a joy, not a burden, for that would be of no benefit to you. (Heb. 13:17, NIV)

We are to submit to those in an authoritative position. We may not like what they are doing. If that is the case, set up a meeting with them and talk it out. Do not spread waves through the body. That is what mere men would do. We are not called to be just mere men and women but to be mighty through God and to be known for our love for one another!

If you hear this going on, you should speak with the person (in love) who is bringing harm to the church. Make them aware of what their words could do to the leadership and how the enemy will try to take full advantage of this situation and destroy the work of the Lord. Also, I would pray for the leaders. Speak life over them and their families. Furthermore, I would share this information with those in leadership. I would suggest that you do not share the names of the one who is creating an issue (that could lead to gossip, and we are trying to govern wrong actions, not throw someone under the bus), but make the leadership aware of what is going on so they can pray as a group and make sure that nothing comes between them due to the negativity spoken over them and their ministry.

> Do not speak against one another, brethren He who speaks against a brother or judges his brother, speaks against the law and judges the law; but if you judge the law, you are not a doer of the law but a judge of it. (James 4:11, NASB)

In studying this passage, I found out that "speak against" has two meanings:

1. To vocally speak negative words out of our mouth
2. To mentally think about these words, meaning to dwell on them

Thinking negative words is just as strong as speaking them out. How so? As we dwell on those negative words, we begin to release a negative atmosphere over our mind. Remember, one aspect of authority is to govern. Have you ever dwelled on something that was negative and it led you to have a bad attitude? Have you noticed that you were negative toward someone who didn't do something wrong toward you? Do not dwell on negativity, or you will begin to speak it out!

The words we allow to "float around" in our mind can cause a spiritual ulcer in our body. Only you can take those thoughts captive. If we dwell on positive things, it will reflect in our walk. The same goes for someone who dwells on negative things. We can not dwell on the negative and exercise kingdom authority, whether in the spirit or natural realm. What are you dwelling on today?

Questions

1. Are you praying for the leaders of your church on a daily basis?

2. Have you, in any way, spread gossip?

3. Are there changes going on in your church? Do these changes make you feel unsettled? Have you met with your pastor?

4. How do you handle the gossip you may hear about your pastor?

5. Are you willing to make a stand for what is right even if it puts your friendship to the test?

12

Authority over Spiritual Mountains

So far, we have looked at what spiritual authority is, who is able to exercise kingdom authority, and how our tongue will either bring life or death to a situation. I would like to explore the positive side of kingdom authority. To walk in true authority found in Christ, it comes down to aligning our faith with His Word. If our alignment is off a degree, then we become off-kilter in the spirit.

> Truly I say to you, whoever says to this mountain, "Be taken up and cast into the sea," and does not doubt in his heart, but believes that what he says is going to happen, it will be granted him. Therefore I say to you, all things for which you pray and ask, believe that you have received them, and they will be granted you. (Mark 11:23–24, NASB)

What a great passage we have as a building block in our foundation. There are a few principles within these verses:

1. "Whoever says to this mountain"—This indicates that we must speak to it!

2. "Does not doubt in his heart"—We have to be secure in our faith.

3. "But believes"—Our faith and hope in Jesus has to be inline.

4. "Believe, and it will be granted"—Just because we pray doesn't mean it will happen; we need to stand in faith to receive.

Our posture before the Lord sets the momentum to overcome! Too many times, we perceive that it is God's problem. He is the answer! Speak to the issue through His name to walk in the victory. Anyone who is in a position of authority has taken the responsibility to stand in the midst of chaos. To speak with authority, we will have to face fear and anxiety and align our trust in God, applying our faith to His will and purposes and not what the world or the enemy has to say about the situation.

This "*mountain*" can be anything from a sickness to a financial burden to issues at your workplace, your home, or among your peers. The bottom line is, we must speak to it in the name of Jesus and confess that we are victorious and stop living a substandard lifestyle.

The second point—"*does not doubt in his heart*"— is such an important part within authority. Think about someone who is in a position of authority. If you sense weakness or doubt in what they are is saying, you may not fully trust them or walk in the direction they are going. We must be confident in Jesus in every aspect of our walk. We cannot confess He is our provider but align our trust in someone to help fulfill our need. Our confession has to line up with the actions we walk in. If your help comes from above, we should set our gaze there first and watch and see how the Lord will use men to help in our time of need. I personally love to see supernatural miracles that can't be rationalized away!

Our doubt will second-guess the ability that Christ is the answer to our need. We have to take authority over doubt and cast it into the sea! *We cannot confess negativity and expect the miraculous!* As we wage war standing in our authority, we need to have a balance in our heart with the assurance that He will grant the prayers that align with His Word and purpose and can bring us further into our destiny.

This passage shows us that we must speak to the mountain, exercise our faith, and hold fast to the promise we have in Christ. We must believe in the prayer we are offering up. (*You may be in a weak place, but you are confessing with a positive, faith-powering prayer to break the yoke of your enemy.*) Your position in a situation may be negative, but your confession is being released through your authority with a positive prospective.

One night as I was worshiping, I came up with this line: "Heaven, come down and rescue me, I won't let go until I am free." I think about this quote at times. Basically my spirit was saying, "Lord, I am calling on your name. I will present myself day and night before your feet until you grant my prayers. I will not stop confessing who you are, and my faith is in you to destroy the works of my enemy. I will not stop presenting my case before you until I am free!" We must not have a beggar's mentality but a worshiper's heart before His throne.

Waging War

As we move in the awareness of our authority found in Christ, there needs to be an understanding of who we are enforcing our authority over. We were not given authority to *change* someone's will but to speak destruction to the enemy that is stopping someone from fulfilling their destiny.

> For our struggle is not against flesh and blood, but against the rulers, against the authorities, against the powers of this dark world and against the spiritual forces of evil in the heavenly realms. (Eph. 6:12, NIV)

This is a clear picture representing kingdom authority. First and foremost, it is exercised in the spirit realm. I am not saying that every issue that comes down the road is from the enemy, so we need to pray for discernment. The Lord is saying, "Stop taking your frustration (*speaking negative words*) out on your peers instead enforce the victory you have in the spirit to push back the work of the enemy. Address your darkness. Declare that his works are rendered null and void in the name of Jesus."

In the natural, if someone stops making payments on their mortgage, the sheriff will send out one of his deputies with an eviction notice. Most cases, it is attached to the front door. We must become a deputy in our land and listen to the sheriff, whose name is Jesus! We must post an eviction notice on every spiritual door that is corrupt and enforce the tenant (the enemy) to leave in the name of Jesus.

The above passage shows us that the enemy has a position in the spirit realm, but we should never give into his ways. Our authority through prayer, declaration, and the actions we take are intended to shatter his ways. Many believers today do not believe in the spiritual battle that we face. This is one of the reasons many are suffering in areas of their life—they are not enforcing the darkness to flee. They are not speaking to the rulers, the powers of this dark world but confessing, "Well, that's just part of life." No, it's not!

The enemy wants to destroy us before we come to the place of understanding our authority and the power we have in the name of Jesus. He will try to destroy us spiritually, physically, mentally, and financially, but through Christ, we have the authority to speak destruction to his camp, and that will bring freedom to our walk! If you are struggling in an area of life, take a step back and think about your prayers. Are you addressing the enemy with your authority or rolling over and accepting defeat?

Mind Games

> For the weapons of our warfare are not of the flesh, but divinely powerful for the destruction of fortresses. We are destroying speculations and every lofty thing raised up against the knowledge of God, and we are taking every thought captive to the obedience of Christ. (2 Cor. 10:4–5, NASB)

Just as we saw in James 4:11, the Lord has instructed us to *not mentally consider* negative words toward anyone. The passage in 2 Corinthians gives insight that there is a battle that wants to take place in our mind. Our mind controls our thoughts, speech, and reactions. If we do not filter our thoughts, they will become a hindrance and jeopardize our ability to enforce our authority.

How do we destroy speculations and every lofty thing that rises up against the knowledge of God? We are called to have the mind of Christ. I invite you to say this: I *bind* my mind to the mind of Christ. When a negative thought comes in, it is my responsibility to reject it and turn my negative thinking to dwell on something positive.

We must get the Word in us so we have a database to retrieve pure thoughts.

If we dwell on anything that is against the knowledge of God, we are giving the enemy a footstool in our mind. Have you heard the statement, "He dwells on it so much it is eating him alive"? If the world or our enemy can get us to dwell on the negative things, it will begin to derail us from enforcing our authority and taking those thoughts captive. Being a Christian is not for the lazy at heart. There is work to be done to sustain our peace in Christ, but through His grace, He lavishes us with rest!

> Finally, brethren, whatever is true, whatever is honorable, whatever is right, whatever is pure, whatever is lovely, whatever is of good repute, if there is any excellence and if anything worthy of praise, dwell on these things. (Phil. 4:8, NASB)

We should strive to dwell on the positive things in life. As we speak about these positive things or declare the Word of the Lord, it will help us reposition our mind to the right perspective we need to stand in the authority that has been granted.

The dictionary defines *captive* as an adjective that means "obliged or forced to listen, whether wanting to or not." It is our duty to keep our mind in check with the Word of the Lord. Only you can harness the thoughts that go through your mind. Are they negative? If so, how are you dealing with them?

In closing, I want to share an experience I had in October 2015. My family and I were on vacation to see my sister and her new baby boy! What a cutie. Anyway, one day the news was reporting that a category 5 hurricane was going to hit Mexico. Later in the day, I began to notice many believers posting comments on Facebook, but it wasn't so much as like, "Let's stand for the people of Mexico." It was more like, "Oh, she posted this, so I will follow suit."

Something rose up in me that triggered a holy frustration toward this storm and the lack of faith in the posts I was reading. As I was on my bed that night, I purposely said to the Father, "Lord, by faith, I am going to Mexico in the spirit to deal with this storm," and I did just that.

I found myself standing on a shoreline, feeling the wind and spray hitting my face as I was lying in bed. I stood there and spoke to that storm and commanded it to dissipate in the name of Jesus. Instantly I heard the Lord say, "When you get up, you will see that the storm was downgraded to a tropical storm." The next morning at breakfast, I saw the repost, and Mexico was saved, and the hurricane turned into a tropical storm! Are you with me? We can do this and see change through the Holy Spirit as Jesus is our door to travel in the spirit (John 10).

Questions

1. What are some of the mountains you are faced with today?

2. Are you practicing the principles found in Mark 11:23–24?

3. Think about your struggles. Are you fighting flesh and blood (Eph. 6:12), or are you taking captive those thoughts?

4. Are you meditating on Philippians 4:8–9?

5. Do you believe you can move mountains through Jesus?

13

Speaking Prophetically

I saved the best for last! In this chapter, we are going to cover a few points on *speaking prophetically* and why it is needed in the church today. Within different denominations, this topic will usually be a highlighted gift or has been given a bad reputation and not allowed to be exercised in their meetings. It boils down to two basic issues: the way the Lord is speaking to His children today and the way the Word is released to the congregation.

The Lord has given his children the right and authority to speak on His behalf:

> Pursue love, yet desire earnestly spiritual gifts, but especially that you may prophesy. For one who speaks in a tongue does not speak to men but to God; for no one understands, but in his spirit he speaks mysteries. But one who prophesies speaks to men for edification and exhortation and consolation. (1 Cor. 14:1–3, NASB)

My goal is to share in a *nutshell* why we should be listening for the voice of the Lord and speaking with authority, releasing "edification, exhortation and consolation" to anyone! To keep this as basic as I can within one chapter, *prophecy* is releasing the testimony of Christ, which is of divine, supernatural revelation, into someone's life or a situation.

If the Word of the Lord is not being released with power and authority in our land, we can count on the enemy speaking lies to cause chaos within the church and the communities we live in. We do not serve a mute God, but one that is speaking and releasing revelation to His children to build up the church in all areas of life. The Lord is loving, caring, and generous and is there to guide us along the paths that we are to walk on. Our Father desires to speak. Are you willing to listen?

What are some of the negative effects we could encounter while speaking prophetically but not being led by the Holy Spirit and or exercising authority correctly?

1. To misunderstand the Word of the Lord and the revelation from heaven.

2. To speak something in the flesh and stating that it was from Jesus.

3. To think that you are God's gift to the body.

4. To speak before God gives us the okay to release the word.

5. To release negative words (i.e., God may reveal someone's sin, but that is for intercession unless you have a bond with that person).

6. To prophesy the marriage of two people. This could case major issues and rejection. (There are times that He will show His will. Be sensitive.)

7. To abuse our authority while speaking and confessing, "This is what the Lord says" (i.e., in regard to financial support for someone, there is nothing wrong with giving to a ministry if you feel led to, but do not fall for those who say, "The Lord is telling me to have you sow into the ministry).

Anytime someone stands up to speak on the behalf of the Lord, they are standing up as an ambassador saying that they have been given the authority to speak and this is what the Lord has to say. This is true. The Lord desires for us to speak. We must be careful in the way we present ourselves and the Word. True authority is ministered with humility and grace upon our lips and based in love. It is very easy to fall into temptation and gain a false sense of who we are in the spirit. Just because we may prophesy does not make us any more special before the Lord or His church.

I do not want to spend much time on the negative side of our authority within speaking on the Lord's behalf, but we must be aware that any negativity spoken and declared in the name of Jesus will cause a stumbling block and *death* to the one you are ministering to. Be alert and think before you speak on the behalf of heaven.

Positive Affirmation Delivered

So who wouldn't want to hear a word of encouragement from their Father in heaven? Remember in your childhood days, you would do something you thought was a huge deal, like riding your bike without training wheels for the first time and looking back to see the one helping you have a huge smile and give you a hug and kiss and say, "Well done" and "I am proud of you!" The same goes for us today when the Lord speaks. He has a huge smile and wants to express His love for us in a tangible way, so He speaks to us through others!

> The sheep that are My own hear and are listening
> to My voice; and I know them, and they follow Me.
> (John 10:27, AMP)

Are we listening to hear what the Lord is saying today? We may find ourselves in a situation where we need guidance, wisdom, and assurance. Who better to turn to than Jesus? What can we gain by someone speaking prophetically into our life and with sincere understanding of their authority in Christ?

1. Assurance that we are loved and are called the beloved

2. Wisdom and revelation spoken into the situation

3. Your calling, purpose, or destiny revealed

4. A road map for your next step in life laid out by the Lord

5. Clarity within your understanding of the Scriptures

6. Life spoken into that place of hopelessness or death

7. Heartache washed away by the love Christ has for you

8. Chains of bondage broken around your life

9. Your tears changed to gladness

10. Your perception of Christ altered in a way that you see Him as your Father

These are just a few points that can be spoken over someone's life as we minister in authority and power through the Holy Spirit. Our Father wants to show us His love on a daily basis; it is His desire to do so! We should not be afraid of the words our Father has for us. We must "test" what is being spoken to make sure it aligns with the written Word. We must make sure that we test the Word and not cast judgment on the one who is speaking in authority, even if they miss what the Lord is trying to say.

We need to be on guard that the words we say and the signature we use to stamp an approval (e.g., "The Lord says this," "My child," "Hear what the Lord is saying," etc.) are not just what we think someone needs to hear. That is not ministering in authority but in the flesh.

We are able to deliver words in power that should set the captives free and lead someone in the right direction—closer to the heart of the Father. Our words through Christ's authority shall break the shackles that are keeping people in bondage. The Word of the Lord is a two-edged sword—life or death. What part of the sword are you wielding today? Speak life and see someone blossom in their walk with Christ.

In closing, I would like to share a testimony. One day, I went to a restaurant to get a salad (yes, at times, I do try to eat healthy!). As I was waiting for it, I noticed it was taking a long time. I sat there for over twenty minutes! Then the lightbulb went on. Hmm, I wonder if the Lord wants to speak to someone who is here.

There was a lady sitting next to me waiting for her takeout also, so I asked the Lord if He had anything to say to her. I heard the Lord say, "Ask her why she stopped playing her piano." As I turned to her, I just said, "Hey, so how are you today, and why did you stop playing your piano?" She casually stated that she was good and was about to answer the question in regard to the piano, and then I saw her face change, and she looked directly at me and said, "How did you know? I don't know you!"

With a smile, I said, "I know you don't, but the Lord knows you as He gave you the gift to play music." I went on to share with her the word the Lord spoke to me: "Tell her that when she begins to play for me, I will use her music to in ways she never dreamt of as I will use it to be a vehicle to heal sickness and destroy cancer" (1 Sam. 16)! Thank you, Jesus. After I shared this, she had tears in her eyes. I told her that Jesus loves her and is waiting to spend time with her as she turns to Him.

14

Are You Ready?

Are you ready to declare with authority today? Are you ready to see a change in your spiritual walk? Are you ready to see your home come back under control, your church blossom in fulfilling its great commission, your finances get balanced, and your community restored?

As you seek the Lord and align your will with His, studying the Scriptures and listening to His voice, you will begin to grow in ministering in the authority He has given you. It is time to make a stand against your enemy and take back the land you have lost due to the words you have spoken or the words someone has released over you.

The Lord is looking for those who want to make a stand for His kingdom. As you make this stand, the blessings of heaven will be upon your life, home, church, and community. How far are you willing to venture out in the Spirit? Are you willing to have encounters in the supernatural and see the manifestations of God?

This book is to help guide you along your walk in gaining understanding of *your* authority in Christ. We must stay open to hear what the Lord is saying today through His written Word. Begin to apply these principles in your walk. Be aware of the movement of the Holy Spirit to guide and direct your path. My gift to you as an individual can be found in the book of Isaiah:

> The Spirit of the LORD will rest on him—the Spirit of wisdom and of understanding, the Spirit of counsel and of might, the Spirit of the knowledge and fear of the LORD. (Isa. 11:2, NIV)

We must understand that this was spoken over the life of Jesus, but we can ask the Lord to release these six aspects of God over our lives. Begin to call on the Spirit of wisdom, the Spirit of understanding, the Spirit of might, and the Spirit of knowledge and ask that the fear of the Lord be evident in your life.

Being an ambassador of Christ, we need to walk in the same Spirit that Christ ministered in! It is time for the body of believers to take on the full appearance of Christ in the way we present ourselves to this hurting world. By dying on the cross, Christ gave us the authority to enforce His victory over the works of the enemy.

Speak boldly and do not back down until you see the fullness of victory in your situation. As you begin to declare your victory, do not be surprised if the enemy raises its head, trying to derail you. Do not listen to those lies but stay firm in your convictions before heaven. Remember, we must confess positive declarations from a place of victory whether we see it or not in our present circumstance.

Final Closure

Friends, I hope and pray that this book has given you inspiration, assurance, guidance, and a passion to move in the authority of Christ. May the Lord reveal Himself to you as you venture out on this new road in the spirit. Remember that authority in Christ is not just released by the leaders of your church. Everyone who calls on the name of Christ has the right and ability to exercise His power. May the Lord be revealed in all that you do and say. Life and death is in the power of *your* tongue!

There will be times of questioning yourself, like, "Did that just happen?" when you begin to open your faith, believing that you can make a change. There will be those who will not stand beside you any longer, but the Father will bring others who will understand and support you in your experiences in the spirit. Remember, He is a good Daddy and will not lead you into danger but will always show His love in all that He does through you. He allows us to have encounters that have purpose and in doing so, brings a change in your midst!

My final thoughts are, enjoy the ride! Have fun in the things the Lord leads you to do. Be confident in your stance before the Father and men on earth. Explore all that He has for you. Become aware of the angelic host that is sent out to help you in your destiny, and by all means, never go back to living a life that is subpar to the one you were truly called to live!

Much love,
Les Tomlinson Jr.
On Fire Ministries

About the Author

Les and his wife, Crystal, have two young daughters, Makayla and Shelby. They live in New Jersey, where Les is the operations manager of a construction surveying company. Les has been in church ministry since 1999. He served as the youth leader for the Assemblies of God for six years. He has ministered in many different aspects of the church—from teaching on the prophetic, intercession, worship, and operating in the authority of Christ.

Today, Les and his family are members of Living Springs Global Fellowship in Hammonton, New Jersey. He participates in teaching on different aspects of God and the gifts we have as believers. Also, he travels to different venues as a guest speaker on Sunday mornings or in conferences.

Les has a passion to share the Gospel and to teach the church the different ways that God speaks to His children. He has a vision to be one who helps leaders equip the body, to see them grow in their calling and help them walk out their destiny. He has a heart to see the body of Christ walk in her full potential.

God has put a hunger in his heart to see revival come and the salvation message spoken wherever he walks. He has a vision to see the local hospitals, bars, and nightclubs to be cleared out due to the power and presence of God in his city.

He hopes as you read this book, there will be a stirring in your spirit to operate in the authority of Christ to see spiritual mountains move, the sick healed, demons cast out, and, Lord willing, the dead be raised for God's glory. Be blessed and walk out your purpose in Jesus's name!

listen|imagine|view|experience

AUDIO BOOK DOWNLOAD INCLUDED WITH THIS BOOK!

In your hands you hold a complete digital entertainment package. In addition to the paper version, you receive a free download of the audio version of this book. Simply use the code listed below when visiting our website. Once downloaded to your computer, you can listen to the book through your computer's speakers, burn it to an audio CD or save the file to your portable music device (such as Apple's popular iPod) and listen on the go!

How to get your free audio book digital download:

1. Visit www.tatepublishing.com and click on the e|LIVE logo on the home page.
2. Enter the following coupon code:
   c556-184b-3fe2-0878-3485-0b68-fa43-5cee
3. Download the audio book from your e|LIVE digital locker and begin enjoying your new digital entertainment package today!